A COLLECTION OF STORIES
*weaving* THE FABRIC OF MOTHERHOOD,
WOMANHOOD & HUMANITY

# woven

YGTMEDIA CO PUBLISHING

"This book is powerful. I felt the emotional energy of these women as I read each of their stories of vulnerability, love, and courage. *Woven* is a wonderful example of what the world needs now—our collective feminine energy—women coming together, supporting each other, listening to each other to learn, heal, and wake up the world. Allow these women to be the light for you, to inspire and encourage women everywhere to speak their truth and follow their heart to live in faith and love. Open your heart and mind and embrace yourself for an emotional and empowering journey of womanhood. You will be grateful you did."

*-Danielle Amos, Millionaire Mentor - The Mindset Coach for Women | Host of the Prosperity Practice Podcast | IG: @_danielle_amos_*

"As we cautiously emerge from a pandemic that demanded women dig deeper and do more with less, this book is a welcome salve. Each contribution provides a raw, heartfelt reminder that women are so much more than the roles we choose and those thrust upon us."

*-Dr. Taryn Taylor, MD, PhD, FRCSC | Assistant Professor, Department of Obstetrics & Gynecology | IG: @drtaryntaylor*

"As an elderly male—although life-long feminist—I'm an outsider to the stories of motherhood longing, pregnancy failure, and birthing ordeal. However, as a father/grandfather, I related absolutely to the love and pride in offspring and was inspired by the indomitable will of the writers to overcome trauma and failure and resistance to evolve into the whole entities they are becoming."

*-Allan O'Marra, Fine Artist |Art Teacher | Curator/Jurist |Writer | IG: @allanomarra*

"Synchronicities are magical when they resonate on levels that speak to our present emotions and experiences of self-reflection, acceptance, and change. *Woven* is a must read as a collection. It has never been more crucial for women to share their significant stories."

*-Georgia Fullerton, BA, ExAT, Master Art Guide | Mentor | IG @createmyartstory*

"This book is just the type of literature that speaks to the many dimensions of what it means to be a woman—the beautiful, the brutal, and the bold new ways we are defining ourselves. We can all find ourselves within these pages."

*-Meg MacPherson, Founder of Phit Physiotherapy, Co-Founder of Articulate Design Co. | IG: @phitphysiomeg @articulatedesignco*

"*Woven* speaks a heartfelt common language with words of compassion and awareness, inviting every woman to discover her power."

*-Lorna Waters-Tellez, RN, BSN, MPH, CCE, IBCLC Aqaba Lactation Consultant/ Childbirth Educator*

"*Woven*. I'm never at a loss for words, but in reading this book, I was left speechless! My heart was so full after I read chapter by chapter, my eyes overflowing with tears, both happy and sad. My soul was full of the magnitude of the words I was so lucky to read in this book. Wow. A must-read for women everywhere. Grab your tissues. Grab the fire in your whole being. This book is about to change your life! Drop. The. Mic!!!! Bravo to these amazing women for bringing this book to life!!!!"

*-Lori Mork, Best-Selling Author | Women's Health and Wellness Coach| Host of the Kiss My Curvy Assets Podcast | IG: @lori.mork*

Published in Canada, for Global Distribution

by YGTMedia Co.

www.ygtmedia.co/publishing

To order additional copies of this book:

publishing@ygtmedia.co

Developmental Editing by Tania Jane Moraes-Vaz

Edited by Christine Stock

Book design by Doris Chung

Cover design by Michelle Fairbanks

Illustration Shutterstock©CoCoArt_Ua

ePub & Kindle editions by Ellie Silpa

Printed in North America

A COLLECTION OF STORIES
*weaving* THE FABRIC OF MOTHERHOOD,
WOMANHOOD & HUMANITY

# woven

## TANIA JANE MORAES–VAZ

CHIARA FRITZLER . KATHERINE EARL . JAKE LEISKE WILLIS . SHARANA ALI
SARA COSTA . PATRICIA MORGAN . KIM SORICHETTI . SONALI THAKER
LISA TOWN . AMY SYED . JENNIFER DE ROSSI . MICHELLE NICOLET . LEANNE FORD
EMILY EDWARDS . PARASTOO BOROUMAND . SHERRI MARIE GAUDET

# Contents

# Introduction

When Sabrina and I first chatted about the idea for this book, it was 2020, in the heat of the summer, in the heat of la revolution and a global upheaval of all the things that have been within plain sight for centuries and generations. Much like how a veil rips to shreds thanks to daily abrasions and wear and tear, the wounds that had been glossed over and suppressed for generations came up for air to breathe, to heal. The veil started to come undone last year. No more would it hold. No longer is performative behavior acceptable. No longer is it okay to simply be informed. The collective consciousness was evolving and rising. World over, there was change in the air. The pantomime had begun, but along with it, it unveiled many truths hidden in plain sight. It gave people the time to collect their bearings, to evaluate and assess the state of their life and well-being. It also brought to light disadvantages and systemic injustices and abrasions that are faced by humans who are BIPOC within our own sub-ethnic communities and the larger collective. It was a year that begged us, as humankind, to be educated, to do the damn work ourselves and examine where our own deep-seated sociocultural beliefs play a role or give us a hand in either being the gatekeepers of things or the ones who are still fighting for their voices to be amplified, to be heard, to be felt and understood. It was an eye-opening moment. We thought, *What if we had a book where we **did** talk about everything that has been swept under the rug—generational healing and trauma; stories of immigration, disruption, and transformation; stories of narratives that are passed on from one generation to the next; stories of what it takes to actually be the healer in your family, what it takes to be the person who breaks the cycle in your family.* And so here we are today.

*Woven* is filled with incredible stories of growth, manifestation, and intergenerational healing and change. The people we are surrounded with, the circumstances we experience, how we think, how we speak, and how we act thereafter influence the state of our life, the state of our being and consciousness, which doesn't mean that pain, hardship, injustice, and darkness do not exist. If anything, darkness has always existed within us and around us. It pervades our daily life, in plain sight. The question becomes: **Are you brave enough? Are you bold enough to see it, acknowledge it, and thereby release whatever power it holds over you and who you choose to be in each moment? Are you brave enough to break the proverbial ice, walk through the fire, and see the transformation that awaits you, if you let it?**

Within the pages of this book are heartfelt words from women who are thought leaders—women who navigated some dark nights of the soul, if you will. They had to have their awakening come about them. They had to be woken. They had to be shaken up in order for any stagnancy to leave their life. *Woven* is not just a journey of changing generational narratives, it also talks about how those narratives influence who we become, how we behave, how we interact with people, how we show up in relationships— personal and business. The narratives we allow into our mind consciously and subconsciously influence our ability to transcend the sociocultural, mental, and emotional limitations woven into our individual stories. Each woman's story talks about the power within our womanhood and motherhood, power that we have inherently within us, yet it still feels like an uphill battle more days than none—all of which came to light over the last year and half. Though we have made advances in women's rights, the misogynistic undertones still color the very fabric of our existence. And still, we are here, persisting, fighting, and forging our path. Though we come from diverse backgrounds and sociocultural experiences, and our stories are intricately different from one another, the undercurrent of emotions that sweeps through them, that lashes out of our soul like waves crashing on seashores and mountains, are one. Our emotion is what connects us to each other. Our stories heal and connect us to each other. Every story has its own texture, feel, and dynamic, yet it is intricately woven together as a global tapestry that unites us together. As you read this book, you will find yourself whispering to yourself, *I see you, I honor you. I am you, and the light in me sees the light in you.* I invite you to read with an open mind and an open heart and to take what it is that you need, whatever it is that you're looking to receive from these beautiful words in this book and apply it to your life.

# I AM Woman

I am woman.

I am mother.

I am the keeper of many secrets.

The lover who loves unconditionally.

The healer who heals with her words, her energy, her touch.

My body is the place of many battle scars—seen and unseen.

I am woman.

I am a warrioress.

I am a creatrix.

I birth life and I nurture it.

Within me lies the power to destroy anything that threatens the very existence of this delicate balance, this fiery tango of divine masculine and feminine.

I am woman.

My tears carry the blood, sweat, and tears of the women who've gone before me.

My shoulders carry the weight of the generations who will go after me.

For them, for me, for us, it is up to me to go first.

To love and respect myself—mind, body, and soul.

To follow every desire audaciously, freely, intuitively.

To forge onto paths never taken before.

To lean into deep self-trust.

To know that within me lies a portal to both worlds.

To know that within me lies the power to love, heal, create, destroy, and bring about a reckoning so strong, life will spring anew.

To know that there is wisdom within me that I cannot fathom, wisdom given to me from God above.

To know that in deep faith lies my confidence, my trust.


I am woman.

I am her.

I am you.

I am me.

And together, we can heal and change the course of things.

*woven*

Lean into your inner divinity, your light, your expression, your deep truth.

*Section 1*

# Worthy of It

Chiara Fritzler

Katherine Earl

Jake Leiske Willis

Sharana Ali

*"Because you're worth it . . ."* a popular tagline we have come to know and love, courtesy of L'Oreal Paris. We devour the ads and the targeted marketing that dictates just how much we are worth, no matter the brand of makeup, skincare, haircare, clothing, or even health and nutrition.

Every single thing that surrounds us asks us to determine our worth . . . buy from our worthiness . . . and if we don't do something, we lack self-worth. It's become the buzzword of our generation, along with self-care and self-love.

But what if we entertained this new thought: What if we are worthy just as we are? What if we have already arrived in all our glory the day we came here earthside? What if we were already enough—without the titles, without the brands, without the fluff and frills, the appearances and obligations?

*woven*

Makes you think, doesn't it? Our worth is something inherent within us, yet it gets chipped away, bit by bit—through words, behaviors, family/societal/cultural/religious expectations, and more. Through comparing ourselves to the picture-perfect highlight reel we see online. To the incomes, homes, cars, and, of course, the growing families around us.

What if, just what if, we stopped allowing all of that to dictate our worth? Who are you? Who would you be? What would you do? What would you stand for? What would be a standard, no longer an expectation? How would you show up?

Your worth does not lie in the income you make, the clothes you wear, the titles and roles you play, the children you have or don't have. It doesn't depend on your relationship status, your sex life, or your family's "peanut gallery" feedback and opinion of how you "should" live your life. Your worth is not tied to anyone who chooses to demean you, belittle you, and crush your spirit. It is not tied to anyone who chooses to project their limitations and beliefs onto you. Nor is it tied to what anyone thinks of you.

What if you believed in the catchy tagline and lived your life as if you're worth it. All the time. Every time. Because you are fucking worth it. So start reclaiming it, one piece at a time. In a "no" or "yes." No more "It's okay," or "it's fine," when it's not fine at all. Reclaim it in how you show up, how you share your story, how you speak to yourself about yourself, who you allow into your life, your mind, your heart, and your soul. And most importantly, how you love yourself and allow yourself to be loved. You are worthy of receiving your heart's desires and nothing less. You are here to end the cycle that continued to repeat itself until it collided with you. It may have started from your past, but it ends with you. Here's to you rewriting old stories and narratives, standing in your worth, and owning who you are, unapologetically!

*woven*

# A Reclamation of Worth and Sovereignty of Self

Who are you? Underneath all those titles, all the capes you juggle, all the fancy everything . . . Who are you? I really want to know . . .

Because learning to come home to myself didn't happen overnight, it has been an UNlearning, UNbecoming, and UNfurling of who I thought I needed to be, had to be, who I "should" be.

When all I needed to do was . . . be ME.

Unapologetically. Confidently. And shine my light so others also have the courage to do so.

We women, we are powerful and strong. Majestic. A force to be reckoned with.

As you read this, I want you to know that you are desired, worthy, enough, loved, and most certainly not too much.

Let your roar continue. Let it get louder.

The battle cry continues to rage on . . . until

She is heard,

She is revered,

She is cherished.

Only then can you harness Her energy.

Sweet soul, you cannot expect the world to give you respect, love, honor, and anything else you desire unless you give that to yourself, to Her, to your Wild Child. Your Divine Goddess.

Witch. Crone. Maiden.

Mother. Seer. Sage.

Goddess. Wisewoman.

Bruja. And more.

Silenced through the ages. Burned at the stake. Skinned and plundered.

And even today, She is silenced.

So often, we dim our light, our voice, our sovereignty, our feminine energy, our strength to appease others, when in fact, ours are the waters that nurture, nourish, replenish, create.

Ours is the fire that burns to the ground what we once

thought we wanted or needed, only to create something from the ashes and rise up like the phoenix we are.

We suppress our truth, suffocate our desires, snuff out the flame that burns bright within us . . . to keep the peace, to fit in, to get through just one more day, one more week, one more month, one more year.

To that I say, no more.

Roar, louder than ever—with your energy, your actions, your words, your thoughts, and your desires.

Listen to Her. Seek Her.

Stoke your flames. Let them burn brightly and pave the way.

Stand tall and powerfully in your grace, strength, and sovereignty.

Evolve; it's inevitable that you will.

Rise, because you have been called to do so.

And hang on to the facets that make you who you are.

# Chapter 1

# The Tarnished Crown

Chiara Fritzler

*Chiara Fritzler*

Chiara Fritzler is a writer who loves old books, red wine, and Hawkins Cheezies. Her blog, *All of Your Baggage Should Be Carry-On—Stop Feeling Sorry For Yourself and Find Your Joy*, was created to help others realize that they aren't defined by their diagnoses, past, job, or any other title they may have placed on themselves (or that others have given them). Chiara innately and deeply "feels" her life while she goes through it, and for most of her life, she has felt pressure to suppress her naturally outspoken nature and drive to lead. A forty-something single mom to a toddler, she has navigated polycystic ovarian syndrome (PCOS), weight issues, anxiety, depression, job loss, infertility, and divorce, and she refuses to give in to the pity of *"why me?"* and instead focuses on *"What am I meant to do with the place I'm in?"*

🌐 carryonchiara.com

📷 @carry_on_chiara

To the women who feel like their worthiness lies in their busyness. Find truth in realizing that moments of quiet reflection and times of boredom can lead to the greatest growth and unburden yourself from the pressure you put on yourself and your family. If your busyness is your way of avoidance, take the time to acknowledge and conquer whatever you're avoiding. I hope you come to learn the difference between hard work and heart work, and how you can do both.

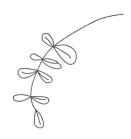

"Somehow, somewhere, we lost the truth that doing nothing is doing something and that our best achievements can come in moments of quiet stillness."

# The Tarnished Crown

*Beware the barrenness of a busy life.*
–Socrates

I've bought into it. I've subscribed to the newsletter, the monthly magazines, and the weekly emails, and I've joined the book club. "Busy" has been my response to the question, "How are you?" I have fully immersed myself into the notion that busy = worthy . . . and where has it got me? Nowhere.

Wait. That's a lie. I've absolutely progressed with this notion. I've moved leagues toward a goal. It's just a terrible, useless goal that is in the opposite direction of where I actually want to be and where I'm at my best.

I have achieved the goal of being an empty, spent shell, strutting around like it made me someone worth admiring.

We have been told that we need to give of ourselves until there is nothing left to give. The media, our friends, social media, television shows, they all say the same thing. It has been reinforced that unless you are tired, busy, or overwhelmed, you're not doing enough and aren't worthy of the skin you're in. Oh, and throw in the "single parent" part of that (I'm a single mom) . . . we've got a completely new breed of absurd expectations about how much we should give of ourselves. Sure, I've got a full-time job, a writing career, a toddler with me most of the time, and then "life," but does the fact that I haven't found a proper balance with these things make me some sort of bizzarro hero in peanut-butter–stained pajama pants with gray roots and dark under-eye circles?

I'm part of a number of groups of women who abhor the "self-deprecating" or "over-giving" camp of thought, and who fight it with every ounce of their being. These people constantly talk, post, and market the concept of giving *to* yourself, not *of* yourself. "We need to fill our own cups first because you can't pour from an empty cup." I'm sure you've heard this sentiment too.

Do I understand it logically? Yes.

Can I commit to it emotionally or mentally? Well, let me tell you where I'm at . . .

I am so spent, I can't cry. Multiple times a week I have this inner sense that if I could just have a good cry, I would release so much tension and so much angst, and I would feel lighter and less burdened. But I can't. I've tried sappy movies (I HATE chick flicks and overtly sad movies, so watching them shows how desperate I am). I've tried ruminating over the stuff in my life that didn't go as I wanted, and I've even thought about major life losses—to no avail. I've had small cries over things that might happen in my life twenty years from now (like how my toddler will grow up and I'll be alone); a super useful way to expend time and energy, I know. But nothing releases. Nothing feels better. Nothing gives. There is Nothing. Left. To. Give.

Or maybe I'm just dehydrated? Perhaps I should add water to my daily liquid intake of coffee and wine. Hmm . . . would that help me cry? But onward with the "nothing left to give" business.

I am not sharing about my emptiness or inability to cry because I'm proud of it. Or because I want you to look at me and think, *Wow, she gives so much of herself. How amazing.* No. It's stupid, ridiculous, and irrational, but I am having a hard time stopping. I really struggle with anything that I think is "half-assed" or that I can't commit to fully. *If it doesn't take from me, is it even worth it?* I used to be very close with someone who thought that the idea of going for a walk was ridiculous. Even a slow jog was pointless because if you were going to exercise, for goodness' sake, you were going to run hills until you barfed or lift weights so heavy you would pass out. I was fully on board with this mindset; I used to be a part of something called "Soldiers of Fitness," where we exercised outdoors, no matter the weather. I live in Calgary, Alberta, so that meant sometimes it was minus forty degrees Celsius and sometimes it was thirty degrees. We didn't use normal exercise equipment; we used truck tires, rebar, heavy-gauge chains, and telephone poles. After one such workout, I stopped at a convenience store to get some Gatorade because I was feeling especially depleted, and I was so drenched in sweat that the person behind the counter asked me if I had been swimming. I LOVED this exercise. It took everything I had. I was forced to push beyond what I thought I could do, and I accomplished more than I thought possible. I left each session barely able to move or think straight, but I had a huge smile on my face and a feeling of pride.

But the point of this exercise group wasn't simply pushing individual limits; a huge part of it was being part of a team. You could rely on those around you to hold you up, pick you up, or do what you simply could not. If the warm-up consisted of eighty push-ups and I was only capable of twenty, my fellow "soldiers" would say, "Fritzler, I got ten for you" or "I got five for you" and so on, until my eighty were accounted for. We were a team, and we never let each other down. We struggled together and came through together, no matter what it took. Nobody was ever left behind. We had a community. Kinship. The feeling of family and belonging.

I seem to have forgotten the concept of how you need a team, a group, and those who are willing to give some of what they have

*woven*

in order to help achieve a goal. I've been trying to do it all myself, and although everything gets done, I'm failing myself. And when failure isn't an option, I just keep pushing myself further until I get to that point of being unable to cry.

I follow someone on Instagram, maybe an online personality or influencer. This woman is around my age and is going through a divorce as well, though more recently than I. She is constantly posting about how her friends rally around her and how she has this incredible community of people. They have rushed to her side and become the supports for a crumbling wall, ensuring that it stays stable in times of distress. I don't have this huge community of support, and sometimes I find myself envious over the fact that she does. I have amazing friends, and they have supported me through a lot, but it's just not the same. I have friends who bought a place in a small community north of Calgary, and many of their closest friends bought acreages in the same crescent. They hung out all the time, and watched their kids grow up together, while they poured love and caring onto each other. I see posts where women talk about their fierce lady friendships where they believe in each other no matter what. And I feel like I don't have as much of that as I'd like. But I'm learning why with the support of my therapist (I think everyone should have a therapist).

I'm not asking you to have a pity party for me. These women didn't sit in a cave and feel sorry for themselves. They actively pursued relationships and a) found a group of people who will love them, and b) stepped away from the martyrdom of doing it all themselves. They don't superficially say, "It takes a village" as a trite slogan. They live it. I, on the other hand, keep trying to do it on my own, pushing through and attempting to prove something to someone. Whoever that someone is, I hope you're thoroughly impressed. Because it is all kinds of stupid over here, the things I'm doing. And despite much evidence to the contrary, I truly don't want to do it all on my own anymore.

And now, I need to acknowledge something that might come across as contradictory, but I'll say it anyway. I've seen a lot of (what I think is) nonsense about how "overwhelm is a choice." This kind of rubbish seems to come from people who have a lot of privilege, either monetarily or through support. Those who say those types of quotes have no idea what it means to not have a stable, supportive, second adult in your home to relieve you from everyday mental and financial stressors. They don't know the tears that come at night because of the burden of not having reprieve. They clearly don't understand the single-parenting issue of not being able to tag team with someone when your child needs more than you have left to give. They're deluded about the luxury of being able to go for a walk alone to decompress or even having a quiet bubble bath. So, to the next person who says another parent is overwhelmed because they're choosing to be or implies a parent can't afford what they're selling because they just haven't properly allotted their income: C'mon over and ring my doorbell for a "Welcome to reality" conversation. We'll have a little chat about the guilt and shame that you're projecting onto women who are doing their best with what they've got. And I'll clarify that sometimes our "best" means we don't have the time, bandwidth, or extra income for whatever you're trying to sell us.

There is no reward for this exhaustion. There is no one to applaud us for being busy or overwhelmed. If you have children, you know that all they want is your time and attention ("look at me, Mama!"). That ridiculous crown a la *Coming to America* (one of my absolute favorite movies) that we've given to ourselves, it's crooked, tarnished, and covered in dollar-store plastic jewels. If your toddler made it for you, it would be beautiful, but wearing it everywhere like it's some sign of moral or ethical superiority is preposterous. We need to get over ourselves. No, I have not chosen the overwhelm, the busy, or the exhausted, but I am also not doing everything I could do to manage it a little better.

Here are the things I've heard (and try to tell myself):

Put down your phone.

Stop checking social media.

Don't check your work email at night.

Give yourself a mini break.

Go for a walk and/or do at least thirty minutes of exercise a day.

These types of suggestions used to irritate me a lot. Do you know why? Because I wasn't doing them. Heck, I'm still not doing them. I'm working toward these things and making the tiniest but mightiest bit of progress. I don't watch the news anymore, and I rarely go on Facebook. Neither of those things ever brought me joy, and I always left them feeling worse about myself, or the world, or both. It was tough to quit Facebook, especially now with it being a source of "connection," but none of it felt genuine to me. I would look at people's profiles and compare my life to theirs. I know deep down there is a lot I can do to better myself physically, emotionally, and mentally, but I still struggle with where to begin, so those aforementioned comments just made me mad. I figured, "You can't understand where I'm at, and if one more person tells me to take a stupid bubble bath, I'm going to outright lose my mind."

Instead, here's what I decided for myself. I've decided that twice a year, I'll go away on my own for a few days. I did it last fall, and it was amazing. I came back feeling like a completely different person, like a previously empty vessel had been filled—not completely, but with enough to give. Interestingly, though, part of me actually felt a bit more impatient and intolerant when I returned. It's almost like I resented having to come home and get back to reality. Perhaps I subconsciously wanted to protect my resources and prevent myself from being drained again because I

*woven*

knew I hadn't set up my life to stop it from happening. I missed my daughter, my familiar home, and my cat, but I was cranky about coming home. I want to acknowledge that if you also feel this way after a break from your kids or life or whatever, you're not alone. And if it's weird to feel that way, we can be weird together.

The strange concept of worthiness being tied to busyness baffles me. Where did it all start? Being busy doesn't mean we're being productive! Somehow, somewhere, we lost the truth that doing nothing is doing something and that our best achievements can come in moments of quiet stillness. This belief, of course, requires us to reframe the idea of "achievement" and believe that attending to our mental health and setting a good example for our children are worthy achievements. I want better for my daughter. I want to break the generational idea of busy = worthy. She's already a very "busy" child, almost always on the go. But she also has wondrous moments of quiet, singing to herself or telling herself stories. My mom has been a big supporter of my desire to be less busy, and she reminds me how quickly children grow up and the short amount of time we have with them when they're little. She worries that I will have regrets and guilt, but I remind her that it's unlikely there's one mom in the history of time who got out of life without regrets or guilt, regardless of how much time they spent with their children.

The ridiculousness of being busy isn't new. In Soren Kierkegaard's

1843 treatise, *Either/Or: A Fragment of Life*, he writes: "'Of all ridiculous things the most ridiculous to me, to be busy . . . What, I wonder, do these busy folks get done?' Are we too busy to *truly* live our lives because we're not present in them? If we're constantly busy, when do we reflect on the purpose of our life, who we are, or how to be true to ourselves? Will our final moments in this life involve thoughts of 'I wish I had been busier?'"

So, let's take off our tacky, tarnished crowns of ridiculous expectations and false exultation. Let's find some sort of awful display case that we can put them in, and when we walk past, we can say, "Yeah, I wore that for a while. It was heavy, and I thought it was beautiful and made me important. But really, it never impressed anyone."

# Chapter 2

# The Alchemy of Self-Love

KATHERINE EARL

*Katherine Earl*

Katherine Earl is a certified teacher, nonprofit program director, visual artist, author, and mother of two. Over the span of fifteen years, Katherine has conceptualized and brought to life more than 200 community programs, events, and performances that empower young people to address community needs using the arts. Her most recent accomplishment is creating *My Life Playbook*, an arts-based creative journal for kids that promotes self-awareness, self-love, and mindfulness. The success of *My Life Playbook* inspired the birth of Katherine's business, My Life Creative, a blog and online store that sells arts-based products that help build confident and resilient kids. Katherine has been a guest expert on CBC News, CTV News, and Global News where she has talked about how we can support children by teaching them mindfulness and self-love through fun and engaging activities. Katherine prides herself on merging the arts with personal development and has a particular interest in the intersection between creativity and building resilience in children.

At home, Katherine is a yoga enthusiast who is at her happiest when hiking through the forest. She loves dancing in kitchens, sipping her favorite cheap wine, and going to bed at a reasonable hour. Katherine's life mission is to use the arts to create fun and interactive experiences that promote resilience, emotional well-being, and personal growth in everyone, but especially children.

🌐 mylifecreative.com

📷 mylifecreativekids

♪ @mylifecreativekids

I dedicate this chapter to the fierce females in my lineage, past, present, and yet to be born. We are all a part of one another's stories. May we move with our collective power and grace.

" . . . *every seed* we plant in our minds and hearts grows, much like the seeds we plant in our gardens at home. Self-love, forgiveness, mindfulness, worthiness, and gratitude are much like that. What we focus on, fixate on, and give our energy to expands."

# The Alchemy of Self-Love

*If we give our children sound self-love, they will be able to deal with whatever life puts before them.*
–Bell Hooks, Teaching to Transgress: Education as the Practice of Freedom

We all have them. The stories of unworthiness that stem from our childhood that begin with offhand critical remarks or insensitive comments made in our formative years.

"You're too much."

"You're too sensitive."

"You think too much."

"You're so scattered."

"You talk too much."

"You're such a daydreamer."

"You have your head in the clouds."

"You can't do *that*."

"*You* can't do that."

The list goes on and on. No matter how minute, these comments plant the seeds of unworthiness that continue to grow within us from a young, impressionable age, and we, ourselves, water them into towering trees of limiting self-doubt.

I come from a family that has always vocalized their love for me. I'm a mother of two adoring girls. I have a partner of twelve years who has loved me through my most awful moments and taught me more about myself than I have been willing to learn. Although I will share some of my darker life-defining moments here, my life has been full of so many blessings and joy. Yet self-love is an everyday choice for me. It's a muscle I need to exercise daily so it can grow stronger with time, so I can be softer with myself and love myself wholly, every single day.

Self-love means loving ourselves even after yelling at our kids for being kids, loving ourselves even when we are stricken with grief and heartbreak. Self-love is also celebrating the wins, owning our inner and outer beauty, and nurturing the needs of our gorgeous bodies. We are too unique, too valuable, and too exquisite and wise to not realize our potential. Who we are and who we are becoming are always results of the seeds that were once planted in us. What we nourish grows. Worthiness, self-love, mindfulness, gratitude, and positive self-talk are all seeds that I chose to plant within myself through different pivotal moments of my life and now weave into my motherhood and womanhood.

## The Seed of Unworthiness

My seeds of unworthiness were first planted when I was growing up as a child in a multiracial family living in a predominantly white small town. I experienced a series of microaggressions early in life before I even knew what they meant. By the time I was ten, I had experienced enough acts of racism that I felt officially othered. When I was four years old, I was taunted by a six-year-old because my parents weren't of the same skin color. I remember kids calling me "blackie" in grade two and the "N word" in grade three. In grade four, I distinctly overheard my crush admitting to his friend that he liked me, only to be laughed at for it. Classmates and teachers inquired, "Where are your people from?" and the classic, "What ARE you?" It was subtle most of the time, but relentless. Ironically, by the standards of my current city's diverse population, many have told me as an adult that I pass as white, which is typical of being multiethnic: you are not quite one or the other and therefore, not enough of either. My young mind knew enough to know that the kids who bullied me weren't coming from a place of malice but rather as the product of generational ignorance and lack of cultural exposure. Since I didn't know how to speak up or who to speak to, I let my feelings of isolation and inadequacy develop into low self-esteem. I still enjoyed solid friendships, sleepovers, crushes, and adventures, but I was certain that none of my childhood friends could tell me where Trinidad was on a map. They weren't eating delicious dahl and rice for dinner, nor did they have leftover roti in their lunch box. They probably weren't spending weekends at backyard jams with big pots of pilau and loud Soca music playing. I adored all my family's unique charm, but I didn't see us represented anywhere. I felt overarchingly unseen and misunderstood, feelings that came to define my identity. When I was a teenager, these feelings were only amplified. I assumed that finding love, having kids or having a career weren't dreams that were available to me. Instead, angst and self-destructive behaviors had me stoned, skipping school, and feeling apathetic 100 percent of the time, which further deepened my lack of self-worth. I wish I had known then that I'd grow up and leave that town, only to find my people, my place, and my sense of belonging, and that I'd eventually come to love myself, flaws and all.

The thing with unworthiness is that it comes to kick you while you're down. While I've had countless blessings in my life, it was during the times when I had to scrape myself off the floor that I learned the most about how to love myself. I was forced to find enough love for myself to simply put one foot in front of the other. After turning forty, I began to release the things in my life that

*woven*

no longer served me (as many of us women do): deadbeat people, clothes that will never fit again, my long hair, and that tired lack of self-love. I wanted freedom from it all! It finally dawned on me that I could *choose* to love myself. I remembered the instances that I had been *shown* love by others. I remembered I was repeatedly *told* that I should love myself. But I don't remember anyone teaching me *how* to practice self-love. I started living unapologetically and intentionally. I created the space to pursue my interests aside from motherhood and wife-dom. I identified and let go of countless limiting beliefs, all by choosing to focus only on the things that supported my inner love quest.

The first time I truly fell in love with myself was at a rave in the late nineties. I was eighteen years old at the time, and in that moment, I was peaking on some MDMA that my best friend had let me snort off her compact mirror in the bathroom of a warehouse somewhere in the seedy armpit of downtown Toronto. I remember lights, music, and a feeling of utter clarity and divine joy. True, it was a drug-induced moment of self-love and was arguably inauthentic, but it was the first time I felt absolutely enamored with myself. I danced for hours with my eyes closed, feeling beautiful, free, and fucking unstoppable. I loved the sweat sticking my baby tee to my back; I loved the sting of the glitter eyeshadow sweating down into my eyeballs; I loved how my heartbeat aligned with the four-on-the-floor drumbeat. I felt connected to my purpose. I knew that all the things I could ever want in life were also desperately wanting me back, that my desires also desired me. It was the first time I realized that loving myself was even a possibility. In retrospect, I do not advise that people chase the feeling of self-love by experimenting with recreational drugs like I did! While I had some good times, the depressing aftermath of getting high outweighed any measure of the love I felt on the dance floor. My sense of inadequacy increased because I realized I could only feel that level of love for myself when I was intoxicated with something. I ditched the drugs fairly quickly, determined to achieve the intense joy I felt on that dance floor without the help of faux fairy wings, Tiger Balm, and little blue butterfly-shaped pills.

## The Seed of Mindfulness

I was introduced to mindfulness in my twenties while I was developing a profound passion for art making, elementary education, and community development. I had a fulfilling job that allowed me to merge all my passions and make money doing it. I was also experiencing an abundance of undiagnosed anxiety. A normal day consisted of me drinking a lot of coffee, eating processed food, overworking, and being consumed by my inadequacies. In the evenings I'd hang with my friends, drink bottles of wine, and have nightmarish sleep. After some time, the joy I once felt in my job was overshadowed by anxiety. I had random panic attacks when my heart palpitated and I had desperate urges to physically escape from my surroundings. I'd look in the mirror, disappointed in what I saw physically and internally. I was physically ill for months at a time, having multiple doctors tell me that whatever I had, they couldn't fix, and that I might just be "unlucky." I fell into a vicious cycle of hopeless, self-destructive behaviors. On a whim, a friend asked me to join her at a weekly yoga class. As I began to connect my physical body with my mind and soul through yoga and mindful breathing, I became motivated to shed some of my negative behaviors and noticed my anxiety dramatically decreasing. I felt inspired to clean up my diet, I gradually reduced my alcohol intake, and I started using breath-work practices to keep me grounded in the present moment. I couldn't believe how quickly my physical and mental health improved!

Being mindful empowers me to be aware of what I'm thinking and feeling in the present moment without judging myself. Releasing this judgment of self has been central to my mental health. Being mindful has also allowed me to manage the moments when I would have been triggered into self-loathing. I take mindful moments right after my child looks me in the eye defiantly and does the exact thing I just asked her not to. Sometimes I practice mindfulness right after I yell at her because I forgot to take a mindful moment beforehand! I will fully join my kids as they intently watch an ant crawl across the ground. I can mindfully eat a bag of chips if I want to, noticing every bit of salty goodness scrape against my tongue and delighting in the sound of each crunchy bite. Mindfulness allows me to keep my anxiety in check while helping me nurture myself and love myself, mentally, emotionally, and physically.

## The Seed of Gratitude

My journey toward self-love, self-compassion, and owning my self-worth wasn't a linear one. Healing is never a smooth journey. There are curves, jagged edges, and deep abysses we need to embrace, fall through, and rise from. But that is what helps us see the light in our darkest moments; it is what helps us forgive ourselves, love ourselves, and plant seeds of gratitude along the way. When I was thirty-one years old and only one year into my current long-term relationship, I became pregnant. We eventually found out that this beautiful baby, who hadn't even made their appearance earthside, had multiple physical disabilities in utero. My partner and I were given the impossible choice to either give birth to a full-term baby who would face a lifetime of physical pain or to terminate the pregnancy and deliver stillborn. We reluctantly chose the latter. Making this decision was my darkest moment. To this day, I question if I was even in sound mind to choose that option. I felt a deep resentment that we were the ones to choose the fate of our own son. After giving birth to a tiny, perfectly still

*woven*

human, my partner and I were pummeled by immediate regret. The sense of shame was so great that for years we lied, telling friends and family that I'd had a miscarriage. The depth of self-loathing and guilt was paralyzing. I cried for six months straight. My partner and I grieved differently and struggled to connect. I lost my mindfulness practice, likely too ashamed and afraid to face my true self. My journal was my only solace. I poured all my sadness, shame, guilt, and more into it, writing until there was nothing left to write. After a while, I forced myself to write down one thing I was grateful for each day, desperately trying to reintegrate some positive thinking into my life. Somedays I could only feel grateful for small things like the warmth of a cup of tea against my cold palms or the way my pen smoothly glided along the paper. Other times I was able to express gratitude for what the loss of our son taught me about myself and my relationships. Expressing my gratitude slowly let pieces of light shine through the darkness. I started to allow myself to receive the generous onslaught of loving kindness from those nearest to me. Gratitude prompted me to accept the truth of our decision despite how horribly ashamed I had once felt and to eventually see this experience as a defining moment in my personal development. Gratitude is a daily practice for me now. It allows me to celebrate all the amazing parts of my life that I could otherwise so easily overlook.

### The Seed of Self-Compassion

I have learned that self-love is connected to self-esteem, which is largely influenced by our mindset. Our brains are wired to see the negative first, so we naturally obsess over our flaws before seeing what makes us unique and amazing. We have to consciously choose to be positive. My inner critic stepped up to the mic when a few years ago my partner of eight years instigated a (much needed) separation and was out of the house a couple days later. She (Ms. Inner Critic) resurrected the feelings from my childhood that said, *I couldn't be loved by people who didn't have to love me.* She blamed the separation on me: *I was too naggy, I was too focused on the kids, and I had too much unresolved baggage.* I was a self-loathing mess for a couple months before I realized that the separation was an opportunity for me to unpack my "baggage" and examine the feelings of unworthiness I have carried throughout my life.

Since my partner and I shared the responsibility of caring for our kids, I had the space to rediscover my identity aside from being a mother and wife. I immersed myself in books and podcasts about worthiness and self-love. I realized the stories I'd been telling myself my whole life were just that, stories. It was a lightbulb moment . . . the stories I told myself were in my own control—I didn't have to identify as unworthy and inadequate! I could rewrite my sense of self-worth. I began to practice affirmations, wrote love notes to myself, and nurtured my body, mind, and soul with healthy foods

*woven*

and a solid yoga practice. I replaced the "I can't and I want" with "I can and I am." I rediscovered my love for art making. After a while, I couldn't hear my inner critic anymore, as I was too busy complimenting myself and feeling fly most of the time! I felt genuine gratitude for my partner's brave decision to ask for the space he needed, and by default, I relished the space I was gifted in return.

I reflected on the things I hadn't taken the time to question— what relationships should and could look like, my role as a mother, and my life's purpose. I challenged the conditions society placed on these things and vowed to live the rest of my life by my own standards. I lovingly let go of our beautiful relationship and lived in the present as the best version of myself. I accepted my new reality, assuring myself that I would be okay no matter what the next phase might bring. Unexpectedly, my partner and I reunited a year and a half later. We consider the separation to be our healthiest decision yet. If I had listened to my inner critic, I would probably have drowned in a river of my own tears, entirely missing the opportunity for any personal evolution whatsoever. Now, I infuse positive self-talk into my daily life. When I'm feeling mopey, I look in the mirror and say, "I choose happiness today." If I don't like what I see in the mirror, I remind myself of how sexy and loveable I am. When I'm feeling underwhelmed by the numbers on my bank statement, I imagine rolling around on silk sheets in a pile of hundred-dollar bills, visualizing the abundance I know is coming my way. The transformation in my mindset has been surprisingly motivating. My inner critic is still there. Her cranky voice is still more convincing than mine at times, but now I know how to put her in place and lead myself toward my dreams and desires instead of succumbing to my fears and doubts.

There you have it, the seeds of homecoming that will lead you home to yourself, who you are, your essence, your worth, your desires. At the heart of it, every seed we plant in our minds and hearts grows, much like the seeds we plant in our gardens at home. Self-love, forgiveness, mindfulness, worthiness, and gratitude are much like that. What we focus on, fixate on, and give our energy to expands, which doesn't mean bypassing our emotions or the hard stuff when it hits us. Instead, there is power in sitting with it, reflecting on it, and allowing ourselves and our bodies the grace to move with it, one step at a time.

When I finally learned to forgive myself, copious amounts of unnecessary shame were lifted from my shoulders. I felt freer, lighter. Self-compassion has become the key to loving myself even when I don't feel worthy of love. Self-compassion is a reminder of our humanness and how our imperfections connect us and weave us together. Like the time my tube top came down to my waist as I was biking down a busy road exposing my bare chest to rush-hour traffic. Or the sinking feeling of regret after sending a steamy text to

*woven*

the wrong person. I think about the times I was slumped drunkenly on the kitchen floor in a puddle of teary heartbreak. Or the deeply pitted guilt I have felt after spitting volatile words I never thought I'd say to my partner or kids. Not anymore! Self-compassion is the golden ticket to letting go and the motivation to do better next time. Now, I can say *hey* to my self-deprecating feelings as though nodding to a passing stranger, letting them stroll on by. Practicing self-compassion has allowed me to replenish myself with pure and forgiving love. It is the alchemy of self-love: turning feelings of shame into tenacity.

If self-love means loving ourselves unconditionally, then I know I'm still on my journey to embodying it to the degree to which I know I'm worthy. I still face daily feelings of unworthiness, guilt, and shame in various forms. I know that we all do and that it is okay. I have also learned that I can cultivate worthiness from within and that I hold the power to transform painful experiences into the very pillars of my self-worth.

I invite us to grant ourselves permission to be humanly flawed. To take all our imperfections and kiss and cuddle them. To collectively acknowledge that life will be full of many magnificent as well as many lousy days. To allow ourselves to worship ourselves every step of the way. Then let's pay it forward by teaching our kids to do the same for themselves. Our kids will undeniably develop their own seeds of unworthiness. We may not ever know what they are or why they exist. Throughout their lives, our kids will unquestionably water their seeds of unworthiness into towering trees of self-doubt in the same ways we did. Now imagine that the seeds they were watering were those of self-acceptance and self-compassion. Imagine they learned about positive self-talk, gratitude, and self-compassion before enduring inevitable hardships. What if they knew HOW to nurture themselves through these situations? We can show our kids love in all the ways that we already do. We can continue to remind them to love themselves inside and out. And most importantly, we can show them exactly how to do it.

woven

# Chapter 3

# The Making of a Unicorn

Jake Leiske Willis

## Jake Leiske Willis

Jake Leiske Willis has worked in the music/entertainment industry for thirty years. She started her musical journey touring with her parents' gospel band, continuing after high school. In the early '90s, Jake founded Canadian Country vocal band Farmer's Daughter and toured extensively as a singer/songwriter. Farmer's Daughter recorded four records, was honored with awards including a Juno and multiple CCMAs for Best Group or Duo, filmed twelve charting music videos, and toured extensively.

Following her highly successful career as an artist, Jake accepted the position of VP of Creative Services for Big Ride Entertainment, an independent Nashville-based record label. Additionally, she worked in artist development and photo and video production.

Jake returned to Canada to assume the position of artistic director for the Toronto branch of the award-winning event company POP Kollaborative. Her role included creating and coordinating elaborate custom entertainment, garnering the wins of STAR, ESPRIT, and GALA Awards.

Currently, Jake resides in Atlanta, Georgia, with her husband, Chris Willis, and daughter, Avalon. After her extensive fertility journey, Jake has found her passion in becoming a Motherhood Manifestation Mentor, supporting women in their pursuit of becoming mothers when they think they've tried everything!

🌐 **thejaketake.com**

📷 **@Jakeleiskewillis**

**f** **@jakeleiskewillis**

I dedicate this chapter to the Unicorn. Thanks for choosing us, Avalon Berlin Willis!

Christopher, you have given me the greatest gift imaginable, the opportunity to be Avalon's mum, and I love you immeasurably. Savanah (Smooks), every time I look at my daughter, I see you too . . . I WIN! I would also like to acknowledge THE VILLAGE: My blood family who supported this unconventional idea, Kim, Fay, Tucker, Rita, and Gerry! Jeanne Willis, my rockstar MIL! Dr. Kim and Jeanne B., Dr. Licciardi, Dr. Anna Rybka (Dr. Sparkle Eyes), Joy, Cynthya, and Danielle. JUST THANK YOU.

"In my memory of being alive, a more perfect moment doesn't exist. We were connected again, and I couldn't take my eyes off that perfect baby girl; she was so freaking beautiful."

# The Making of a Unicorn

*Only those who will risk going too far can possibly find out how far it is possible to go.*
-T.S. Eliot

My body was in shock. I couldn't stop shaking. I mean shaking, like one step away from convulsions and chipped teeth from the force of the chatter. My nurse leaned on my belly, using her body weight to clear the fluid from my uterus. I didn't feel a thing because of the spinal tap, but I knew there was an incision large enough to pull out a baby, and the force she was using seemed crazy excessive to me. The fluid would have come out naturally if I had pushed the baby through my vagina instead of having a cesarean section. The words "naturally" and "normally" had lost all meaning throughout the past three years after undergoing fertility treatments and being pregnant at fifty-one. But the shaking . . . whoa, that was next level. I was about to ask what my body was going through when the doors to the recovery room opened, and in they came, Christopher and Avalon. It felt like an eternity since the two of them left me in the operating room to get stitched up while they took care of all the birthday details. Chris wasn't letting that child out of his sight. We'd heard one too many "baby got swapped at the hospital" stories to separate for a second, although it would be hard to lose that one, as she had so much hair that she didn't look real! The shot of adrenaline from seeing the two of them walk through the door seemed to accelerate my shaking, but then I experienced the most magical moment of my life. The nurse laid that tiny body on my bare chest, and like a shot of Valium to my vein, the shaking stopped, my heart quit racing, and my body went still. I want to be clear here: it didn't subside or slow down, my body just instantly attuned itself to Avalon's heartbeat, her smell, and all of her. I was floating in that moment, my heart still racing rapidly underneath it all.

In my memory of being alive, a more perfect moment doesn't exist. We were connected again, and I couldn't take my eyes off that perfect baby girl; she was so freaking beautiful. Every needle, every year of IVF treatment, every failed transfer and miscarriage, every hormonal rage, heartbreak, invasive procedure, and

*woven*

pregnant bleed, all of it seemed like a blink of "who cares?" with her in my arms. I begrudgingly let go of her for more tests, and bam, my body instantly started to violently shake again. INSANE! I asked the nurse if I was supposed to be freaking out this way. She informed me that because I didn't go through contractions and vaginal delivery, complete with squeezing a baby and fluid out of my body, the message to the brain was that someone had kidnapped my baby and kicked my body into shock. That answer seemed reasonable to me, so I bought it. I trained myself to question everything throughout the past three years of this journey. I'm sure my husband and I sometimes drove our medical team nuts with our questions, but we were firm believers in understanding our medical care.

At this point, you may be wondering how I found myself in the OR at fifty-one, having my first baby. This moment is the place where many stories intersect. The three-decade-long love story of Chris and me is the foundation of it all. Ours was a love story like the one you read about in books (pun intended) and see in movies. It was messy, beautiful, and complicated, and we kept coming back to it and each other; we were somehow bound. Imprinted, if you will. Love can lead you to do some pretty radical things in this life, and our story is no exception.

Chris and I met in 1989 in a touring gospel band out of California. We fell in love and could have gotten married and started our family in our twenties when one usually procreates and lives *happily ever after.* But we didn't. We separated and pursued our own musical careers.

We remained each other's "person." He was on speed dial for all occasions, good, bad, or just to blow an hour while waiting in the airport lounge. Both of our careers were flying; it felt great. Chris was the number one artist in the world of EDM music with his collaborations with David Guetta, and my country band, Farmer's Daughter, was touring 270 days of the year and sweeping awards across the country. We would see each other occasionally, and each time, the connection felt stronger. *What the hell was this between us?* Our meet-ups were equal parts chemistry, history, fun, laughter, ease, and luxury. It was dreamy. Our airport good-byes were Oscar worthy!

Then something shifted. Chris invited me to a wedding in Ibiza, and over dinner one night, he started telling me how he wanted to be a dad, something I had never heard from him in thirty years of knowing each other. He talked about leaving a legacy, passing on everything he's learned about love, career, and life. Meanwhile, I was sipping my adult beverage and thinking, *Wow, what a beautiful side of you that I didn't know existed.* And then, WHAMO: "Jake, I want to be a dad. I love you, and I want to do this with you." I swear, no one has been at the bottom of more slow-blink moments in my life than this man!

Hold the confetti and champagne! I said NO. I know, right?

I was living in Nashville, Tennessee, at the time and had just been offered a dream job for a premier event company in Toronto, Canada. The thought of giving up the security of a career and a fabulous apartment on the thirty-sixth floor of a luxury complex to enter into this relationship, agreement, arrangement, partnership, whatever the eff it was, scared the daylights out of me. On the one hand, it was what I had wanted my whole life. This man, who was the benchmark for all my relationships, was asking me to join him on a fantastic journey, and my heart said, "Yaaaaassss, at last!" but my head said, "Slow down, player, you're not in a Julia Roberts movie!" So, I moved to Toronto and lived in my dream pad with my little dog, Lola, for a year, working with a team of geniuses creating world-class, award-winning special events.

For a year, Chris called me, and we would continue the conversation of legacy, love, and *us*. He certainly knew what he desired and was not about to give up on what he wanted. He made it very clear that he wanted a family with me. Full on, Mr. and Mrs. Willis, living together in Atlanta, Georgia. Understandably, I had questions, but when he stopped and said, "That's what I want, WHAT DO YOU WANT, JAKE?" my answer came out, "I want the same thing."

This moment is when every quote about risk comes into play. I trusted my gut, the Universe, and Christopher that this was our path. It felt ridiculous to continue denying the inevitable. It felt like the Universe was yelling, "Be together already!"

Within one month, I resigned, moved to Atlanta, and began working simultaneously on my immigration papers and our fertility journey! I don't recommend that combo! Oh, AND we got married!

And we lived happily ever after . . . wrong! They say you don't know what you don't know. Well, that was the case for us. I don't think it would have changed our commitment to having a family, but we had no idea what kind of a ride we were getting on, and I believe that is paramount for anyone getting ready to have a baby. I think that is the design of it all. If people knew everything involved (I mean really knew), they might say, "Yeah, no thanks. We're good with Foo Foo, the Pomeranian." Chris and I believed that we would find a fertility specialist, we would pay our money, I would get my shots, and presto-bango, baby! That's not how it rolled out. We were so shocked and devastated when that first IVF transfer failed. It never occurred to us that we would experience that kind of pain once, let alone four more times, until Avalon arrived, who was lucky transfer number six. I suppose in looking back, that's the beauty of it! The ones you least expect to surprise you, surprise you the most. Here's how it rolled out.

Chris and I found our fertility specialist in NYC by referral from a friend who had just gone through the process. We decided right

*woven*

away that we wanted to choose the egg donation route because of the kind of experience we wanted. We were clear that I was forty-seven, and if any rogue eggs were floating around, chances were that they weren't in great shape! So, our specialist introduced us to their database of egg donors. This process was so bizarre! You open the portal and basically input all the traits you want your mama donor to have, including height, eye and hair color, talents like singing, etc. You hit Enter, then all these videos pop up with potential candidates. They talk to you and tell you about themselves. My response to all of them was "Nope, uh-uh. Hell, no. Absolutely not." You get the idea. Chris, at one point, said, "Jake, you are going to have to loosen the grip a wee bit here because no one is going to be perfect, but our baby will be." I learned through this whole process that the moment I let go and allowed rather than forced my will, everything opened up. I got to the place of acceptance in the egg department but still had a very strong hesitation. Call it intuition, an internal pull, whatever, but we discussed using the eggs of my niece Savanah. This subject had come up before, and we faced questions like:

"How weird is this going to be at Christmas?"

"Are my brother and sister-in-law going to feel like this is their grandchild AND their niece or nephew?"

"Is Savanah going to want to raise this child as her own at some point?"

Okay, that last one is kinda funny if you know my niece.

This time was different, though. After all the testing, donor searching, and thought that went into carrying this baby inside me, I wanted my DNA to be part of the equation. So, the moment that Chris and I agreed to ask Savanah, we put a plan in motion. That plan started with a FaceTime with my brother and sister-in-law. If they felt strange about it, we were prepared to move on with our other options and not even approach Savanah. But they were 100 percent behind the plan, so we finished the call, and I picked up my phone to call Savanah. She said yes almost before I finished asking her, and in a matter of weeks, she moved down to Georgia and began getting ready for her egg retrieval.

The following three months were some of my favorite memories. I got to spend time with my niece, whom I have always adored. Seeing her bond with Chris was also so beautiful. I knew that they would love each other, but it was paramount that they build that relationship firsthand. Savanah's DNA was about to be connected to our family forever in the most intimate way, and I didn't want either of them to have any hesitation. Those three months were filled with visits to our integrative medicine doctor for acupuncture and other treatments to prepare us for success (yes, all three of us). We had many long conversations about life and the future, and then there were the trips to NYC to our fertility center, especially during fashion week. It was all so exciting.

*woven*

Savanah was a dream. She had no complaints or concerns about the invasive nature of her role. Hormones, shots, uncomfortable procedures! I mean, seriously, these are the things you do when you are determined to have a baby for yourself, and she did it for me, for Chris and me, for our family. I'll never forget or take for granted the hugeness of this little girl's sacrifice (okay, she was twenty-five at the time, but to me, she'll always be my little Smooks).

The day of the egg retrieval was American Thanksgiving. Savanah and I had sourced out a delightful place to celebrate Thanksgiving dinner. The medical staff informed us that we would be taking Savanah leftovers in a to-go container, as she wouldn't be in any shape to go out after her surgery to harvest the eggs. It's so bizarre to me that we were harvesting our embryo on the day of the harvest celebration! Chris and I were in the waiting room, watching the door and waiting for Savanah to come out of recovery. I remember discussing with Chris how bummed Savanah would be to miss dinner. She had been looking forward to eating at this place for weeks. Then the doors flew open, and out marched Savanah, unassisted, who blurted, "Okay, how long do I have to get ready for dinner?" The nurse was behind her, shrugging. And to top it all off, she gave us seventeen eggs. Yeah, golden goose! It was the best Thanksgiving EVER! We ate, we drank, we celebrated the milestone that we had reached. Chris had made his contribution,

Savanah did her part, and now it was my turn!

Before we left NYC, we learned that there were thirteen viable eggs. Combined with Chris's sperm, we created ten fertilized eggs, and seven of those fertilized eggs turned into embryos that were strong enough to make the journey. It never occurred to us that we wouldn't get pregnant with every one of those embryos. The only question on our minds was *What are we going to name them all?* There I was, still grasping tightly onto this beautiful dream that was now becoming more real with each passing moment. I hadn't yet loosened my grip. How could I?

I began hormone therapy. Chris gave the first injection, and the anticipation of someone else plunging the needle was more than I could bear. I searched "how to administer hormone shots to yourself" on YouTube and began doing so myself for the next couple of years. Strangely, as invasive of an act as it can be, it brought me comfort, likely because it was something I could control. It was interesting and very revealing to discover the things that became validating during this process. Birthing a beautiful creation will bring you to your knees, rendering you both powerful and helpless at the same time, all the while forcing you to lean in in sweet surrender.

Our first transfer was in December. Everything was magical. New York City at Christmastime is a whole vibe in itself. Our emotions were heightened with the excitement of the first transfer.

It's a bizarre feeling KNOWING there is an embryo inside you and the excitement of that life being there. It's like having a juicy secret that is yours alone to hold onto for a while. There was the blessed absence of the deep disappointment in hearing the nurse on the other end of the phone saying, "I have some bad news; we don't have a positive pregnancy test this time." We didn't know at this point what it felt like to fail. Hearing those words, "Failed; failed transfer" were just as painful as a miscarriage. And we experienced these very words four times. I vowed to find another word to take its place instead, as language is a powerful undercurrent that shapes our life and who we are.

There was a beautiful, naïve freshness that we would never feel again after that first trip to NYC for our first transfer. We went on to have five more transfers, of which four of them would not end up rooting themselves in my womb. Through each of these embryo transfers, Chris and I rode the waves of emotion, excitement, confidence, and courage. We immersed ourselves in future-journaling, acupuncture treatments, and Chinese herbal medicine. We were all in. By the time we were nearing our last two embryos, our confidence may have taken a minor setback, but our determination and faith was stronger than ever. We continued to try new modalities, new meditations, crystals—ANYTHING AND EVERYTHING!

With each transfer, my emotions ramped up. I refused to let go of my ironclad grip on ensuring that I became a mother. I recall how I just about lost it when our doctor in NYC suggested we explore surrogacy as an option at the time of our fifth embryo transfer. Somehow I felt that I failed myself and Chris if I didn't carry this baby, and I felt as if I failed our baby. In choosing surrogacy, I would be losing the chance to do all the nurturing things that I planned to do during pregnancy that I read about in all those articles on the Internet. It felt like everyone else did what they were supposed to do: the doctors, Chris, Savanah . . . and for some reason, I couldn't bring it home. Nonetheless, we stayed the course and kept believing, repeating mantras and trying different treatments. I did everything except relinquish my white-knuckle grasp for control in this whole situation.

We often end up seeing the lesson when we are ready, or in some cases, when we have no other choice. During our sixth embryo transfer, Chris couldn't go with me; he had a gig. Mum flew from Canada, and together, we flew to NYC. *Ticktock. Time was ticking. This embryo was the second last. There was only one more left!* This time around, we decided to take the train home on the advice of our integrative doctor. It felt odd not having Chris there. I remember my mother-in-law saying, "Ice cream, Jake, eat some ice cream!" So, this time, I added that to my regime. Looking back, I see the significance of the ice cream. She was telling me to enjoy myself. I was so strict about my diet to the point that

I was obsessive with all things health and superfoods. To me, sitting down and enjoying a lick of delicious, creamy, and sweet ice cream was my way of saying, "Okay, Universe, I'm going to loosen my white-knuckle grip here a little bit and do something different for the sole purpose of bringing a smile to my face." The transfer went smoothly, and we packed up and started our trek home from NYC. The train ride with Mum was just beautiful.

There were nine days between the transfer and the pregnancy test, and those were the longest nine days of my life. The photo of the embryo listed: Embryo 6, one left. *ONE left! OMG, how was there only one left?* It would have been easy to slip into panic and chaos, and all the what ifs, but instead, I woke up every morning and dove into my guided meditations right away to calm myself into a place where I could begin my mantras and "allow." Ah, the word *allow*. Allowance is one of the most powerful words in my vocabulary after this experience. Looking back, it was vital for me to fully understand this word *to be* in a position to parent. I began reframing how I perceived this journey and the outcome and the beauty of every moment of it. I allowed myself to look at our life together with or without a child. I allowed myself to consider the beauty of having a surrogate carry our last embryo for us. I allowed myself to be open to the idea of adoption and to the fact that our family would look like whatever it was supposed to look like. I allowed myself to cry, to be angry, to be scared, to be real. In those moments, I felt safe and connected to the fact that we were going to be a family somehow. *That* was the result I was holding to. The *oneness* I continued to trust in.

Before we knew it, the day to complete my blood work had arrived. Our beautiful team was waiting and were excited for us. Chris and I were excited, but it felt different this time. You know that saying, "Being cautiously optimistic?" Well, that was us. We were quiet. Somber, even. No rah-rah-cheerleader-let's-think-positive attitude. We had a quiet, calm, "this is going to be what it's going to be" energy in this situation. As we finished up my blood work, everyone from the center wished us luck. It's amazing how attached you get to the people experiencing this journey with you. Everyone becomes invested.

Chris and I had a ritual of going out for breakfast someplace lovely after the blood work. We also knew that we had to keep ourselves busy and doing something beautiful, and we took in an exhibit at SCAD FASH. We immersed ourselves in someone else's beautiful, successful creation so that we wouldn't think about ours. It didn't work, as escapism never works. Nothing can distract you when you are waiting for that phone call!

*Ticktock.* The day was passing. Still no word. The later it got in the day, the less hopeful we felt. At 4:00 p.m., we were sitting in our car after arriving home from the exhibit when my phone rang; it was the clinic in NYC. My heart was beating mercilessly fast, and Chris's face was without expression. I answered and put the phone on speaker. The nurse said in a chipper voice, "Hey, Jake, did you get your blood work today? We don't have any results for you." And breathe . . . huge exhale. *What the hell is the Universe trying to do to us? So, all this waiting just to hear that our results were floating around somewhere. But it isn't a hard NO, so there was still hope.* We hung up and just sat in the car in silence while they looked for our intel. The phone rang again. This time, I was lightheaded. I answered, and the voice on the other end said, "We have good news; you have a positive pregnancy test." What. Wow. I couldn't believe it was finally happening! I thanked her profusely and hung up the phone. Chris and I stared at each other blankly. I know—confetti, tears, hugging, kissing . . . all that will be in the movie version. Our real-life response was a silence I won't ever forget.

There are no words to describe what it feels like to be pregnant after a roller coaster of a fertility journey. Throughout my first trimester, I bled every day. Nonstop. Chris was my rock! I needed help keeping calm during those first three months, and I was surrounded. Chris and I built our village over the years, and they now stood circling us: our energy worker and friend, our integrative doctor who was our secret weapon, our doula, our family and friends, and my mindset coach. All these people gave strength, professional expertise, friendship, calm, relief and confidence to our experience when sometimes we could not.

After the first trimester, the bleeding just stopped. Chris sang to my belly every morning, and Avalon began locating his mouth with an elbow or foot. We're not sure whether she was drawn to the sound or saying, "Too loud!"

I loved being pregnant. My connection with Chris continued to grow stronger. As much as my body was experiencing the changes and complications that can come with pregnancy, I reveled in the bliss of my growing belly and the babe within it. One day, Chris and I went in for my weekly checkup with our neonatal specialist, who we had working alongside our ob-gyn because of our "geriatric" pregnancy. (I didn't feel so bad because everyone over thirty-five is considered geriatric.) He was alarmed enough at my blood pressure to admit me to the hospital for observation. When I asked when I could go home, he said, "Most likely when you have the baby." My response was a resounding noooooo. Of course, deep within I knew that it was a call for me to lean into greater surrender. And so, I spent one week in Piedmont Hospital, Buckhead, after surrendering to the fact that it was for our own safety and well-being.

One week later, our doctors collectively agreed that it was time for me to be induced. No sooner did the induction start then Avalon's heart rate dropped—and it wasn't recovering well. We had the option to go for a cesarean section immediately or wait to be induced again the following day. We chose the cesarean. What grounded Chris and me was our music, Oscar Peterson, and then in came our ob-gyn to begin the birth of our beautiful baby, Avalon. None of it was part of my birth plan that we had handed out on crisp pink cardstock paper to all the nurses. None of it was how I imagined it, and yet therein lay the perfection!

I feel her warm, wriggly, tiny body on me. I take in her newborn baby smell. Though she isn't directly of me, she is very much of me, my lineage, my family, my bloodline. And she is all of Chris and his lineage. Our love together. Our stories intertwined together—to make us one. At fifty-one, here I am, a mother to a beautiful baby girl, equal parts me and equal parts Chris. Born in total surrender and grace. She is my proof that miracles exist, that no matter where the winding roads take you, life comes full circle with love and hope. That stories can be powerfully written. That narratives can be changed. That statistics don't mean a thing when you are working with powerful intention, faith, self-trust, compassion, and grace. It doesn't matter *how* your miracles, your gifts, your life's greatest moments and milestones arrive. What matters is the power within you, the trust you have and feel within and around you. You are so supported and surrounded with grace and goodness, and may it be proof that your saving grace, your miracle, your unique rhythm that you dance to in your life is awaiting you . . . are you listening in? Can you hear her call? Lean in. Allowance and surrender will lead you on. And deep, burning faith that the ties that bind your heart will lead you home to yourself. To your miracle. To your unique life song!

*woven*

# Chapter 4

# Forged by Fire

Sharana Ali

*Sharana Ali*

Sharana Ali is the owner and founder of BOSS The Six Edition, a collective empowering individuals (particularly those self-identifying as female) to refine and define their full potential through brunch opportunities and a support system. She is a divorcée and single mother to a strong-willed, confident firecracker who she knows will one day change the world.

By day, Sharana is taking over corporate Toronto, and by night, she's THE BOSS, eating, sleeping, and seeping every ounce of glory from this amazing city she calls home. She is a rose-all-day supporter, and she takes her coffee double-double and as dark as the roast can get.

Through BOSS, Sharana is on a mission to dispel the idea that we need to be on this journey of life alone. Together, through sharing our experiences and stories, we can unite in our emotions. No topic is off the table; if they say it's taboo, Sharana says, "Let's bring it to the table."

This chapter is for the girls who won't because they were told they can't or shouldn't. For the ones who are fed from the fire in their belly and have their eyes fixed on setting the world afire with their magic. This is for my girl, who really is her own.

"The meekness stops with me. The chase for external validation stops with me. . . . The chase for perfectionism ends with me. We, as a powerful mom and daughter duo, are after global domination, of our voice, our Self."

# Forged by Fire

*This is the beginning of you loving yourself. Welcome home.*
-K. Azizian

I had what many would deem a "normal" childhood . . . the type of one you read about in story books. The once-upon-a-time type. Or so I thought. Mom, dad, daughter, and son—we weren't rich or poor. We lived within our means, and yet it seemed like we always had mostly everything we asked for. We weren't spoiled, but we also never went without. We had a roof over our head, food on the table, toys to play with, and best of all, our house was always filled with laughter. Both my parents worked while my brother and I attended school. The only thing missing in our picture-perfect life was the golden retriever in the yard and a white-picket fence.

When I reflect on my childhood, I realize how much went unnoticed by me. My parents, being immigrants to the "true north strong and free," came to Canada for the same reason so many other immigrants do so—for a better life for my brother and me. For better opportunities for us as a family. A move to Canada symbolizes hope, opportunity, and new beginnings to many who move here, and my parents were no different. As a child, I didn't understand or see the sacrifice, the heartache, and the desire or longing to belong. I didn't see displacement, harassment, or a longing to assimilate so fluidly, all so that we wouldn't seem or sound like "outsiders." To me, we were as *golden* as any family that graced the covers of your typical '90's magazine. Whether intentional or not, the "hustle" to *have* it all and *be* it all was extremely well hidden from me as a child. The only real longing I ever had was to visit Grandma and Grandpa's house on the weekend like many of my friends did. The four of us were the only ones from our family living overseas in Canada. It wasn't long before the building blocks of deep longing for validation, acceptance, and connection began to take form—all emotions I would internalize and not once realize that this void would rhythmically repeat itself throughout my life.

Growing up, I was always the "good girl," much like my mom and the women before her. It wasn't even a discussion or question. I played by the rules, went to school, and got good grades. I cringed when anyone "acted out." Whatever anyone's reason for acting out, it didn't matter to me. All that mattered was being the model citizen, the good girl. Nothing else mattered to me except for this one belief that had been so heavily ingrained into me—good will triumph; play by the rules and you get rewarded. I was quiet, and I unintentionally and unknowingly attempted to take up as little physical and metaphorical space as possible. Truthfully, I knew no different. I saw nothing different. In my immediate environment, I saw it play out like a fairy tale: *Put your head down, work hard, keep your emotions to a minimum (or at least within the four walls of your home), and you will succeed.* Looking back now, I realize this mindset was very much a survival one that most immigrant children absorb from watching their parents' journey.

The irony of this paradigm, however, is that my parents weren't "good." Heck, they broke the mold. They moved away from their family to another continent, another culture, another way of being/living/breathing/moving around in society. They worked average jobs for cash before "entering the system"; they rented a basement home. They danced to the beat of their self-created drum, paving a course of their own and living life based on their desires, making me question to date: *Was I "good" and as well-behaved as possible as a means of making it easy for them? Could this behavior have been the beginning of my people-pleasing ways?*

It rang loud and clear (although it was never blatantly spoken) that as a young lady (in direct comparison to my younger brother), it was **my** responsibility to:

1. Lead with love and kill 'em with kindness. And as much as I could, blend in so as to not attract any attention my way.
2. The more digestible and malleable I was, the more likable I would be.

I truly believe that much of this thinking came from seeing my parents doing the same (*mind you, while getting taken on a wild ride many times!*). And so, I listened to my parents and did as my teachers said, no questions asked. I didn't even entertain any other options. When I did dip my toes in hot water, my parents knew exactly how to get me back on course.

I was in grade four, chatting with my best friend on the phone (yes, one with an extremely long cord that was affixed to the wall). We had spent the entire day together yet still had tons to talk about. I remember saying to her, "Let's make a list of all the bad words," and I wrote them all out (I don't know why I did it, but I thought it was cool . . . gutsy even). After the call, I went about my business, doing what most fourth graders did in the nineties. Then, I heard my dad's voice beckoning me to come downstairs.

I walked into the kitchen, my conversation with my best friend and the gutsy move I pulled not too long before all but vaporized into thin air within the recesses of my mind. My dad calmly asked me, "Who's swearing?" and I knew I was busted. How could I have

*woven*

left that list on the kitchen table, darn it! I knew there was no way out but to admit it was me (it was my writing, after all). I owned up. He simply said, "As an educated woman, you have an option of how you express yourself. Either use words to eloquently do so in a respectable way or use curse words to do the opposite." That was it. That was the conversation, and the choice was mine—at nine years old.

The same message echoed: *Kindness. Follow the rules. Be educated. Be better. Act respectfully. Don't be loud. Don't draw attention to yourself. And if you do, you're gambling on how the world will see you.*

And I wanted the world to like me. I wanted to be everyone's friend. I wanted to be digestible. What this translated to, though, was a continuous and arduous search for acceptance and belonging, and not always in the right spaces or from the kindest faces. It created deep codependency between my parents and me, where everything depended on their approval of my choices. And many times, it meant hiding my truth from them, especially if I knew it would disappoint them. It meant being a chameleon and transforming myself into whoever I needed to be to fit in, to be accepted, to belong, to be liked, and (in some instances) to be loved. In hindsight, it meant negating who I was and steering clear of any hint of self-discovery of who I was, what I stood for, and what I was willing to fight for, well into my early adulthood.

Every step of the way, the same message permeated through every fiber of my being. There was no escaping it. I could hear it loud and clear, even when it wasn't blatantly stated:

*Follow the model, and you'll get the results you want . . . ultimately, happiness. Look like them, act like them, be like them, and you will be happy like them.* Like a jingle stuck in my head, my mind repeated these words like a morning affirmation. At the age of seven, it meant counting calories and having a deficit at the end of the day. It meant skipping meals. It meant throwing out my packed lunch and snacks, and trading it all to consume an entire KitKat bar instead. I knew how many calories were in the chocolate bar, and therefore, how many I needed to get rid of by the end of the day. It meant throwing up after dinner. It was the onset of internalizing society's beauty standards without even allowing my body to fully develop, all in complete secrecy and silence. I know this message was NOT the one my parents were instilling in me, and at no time do I blame them for my way of thinking. It was far from what they meant by acting in a respectable, digestible way. But this is how I understood it as a child; this, to me, was within my control when the world around me was teaching me and dictating to me who to be and when.

In high school, it meant trying to dress like the girls everyone liked. It meant achieving good grades and not falling behind in class (because that could never happen) without having anyone

*woven*

around me see me as being someone smart, ambitious, or intelligent (God forbid, I was tagged a nerd). *No. That could never happen.* I would dim my brawn just to fit in for beauty's sake. To be digestible. Palatable. Yes, I walked a tightrope, teeter-tottering on it, praying to God that I could maintain this dual act without losing my balance. Like many rites of passage experienced through high school, having a boyfriend was the most coveted one of all. And this relationship is when my "sugar, spice, and everything nice" demeanor gave way to manipulation, physical and emotional abuse, and a double life.

In front of my family, I was the average teenager. I was trying to work through big emotions, seemingly trying to make my way in the world. They didn't even know I had a boyfriend (and it wasn't even something I had to hide—both my parents would have been fine with it). However, I knew based on how I was treated, spoken to, and the expectations placed on me that my relationship would never have been accepted.

He was a couple years older than I was, and he lavished me with attention (note: not positive attention). I was accepted, and finally by someone other than a family member (who I naturally assumed needed to accept me no matter what). He was in university, well on his way to one day being a doctor. He came from a wealthy family, and he had a car! What more could I ask for as an early teen? Until one day, it wasn't sweet notes, gifts of flowers, or quick pickups on my lunch hour. There was constant pressure to meet his family, amplified harsh tones, an arm grab in public and far worse when it was just the two of us. I knew it was wrong. It was explicit. I never saw this sort of relationship play out—not with my parents, not in the media, not in the stories. And you think I would have spoken up. I didn't. I couldn't. There was no way I wanted to rock the boat. I would rather withstand my harsh reality than draw any additional attention to myself. I didn't want to give up being "one of the girls." I didn't want to be alone and thought I could easily lead this double life based on the trust I built with my family (plus, my parents would have called the cops!). And so, like many in a blatantly toxic relationship, I stayed for more than two years, though things got progressively worse. And my breaking point wasn't even me breaking, it was him. I was in my first year of university when he told me it was over. He had met someone else, and we couldn't be together anymore.

I found myself attracted to toxicity numerous times after that relationship ended. True to word, it was almost like a high. I was convinced I could fix their wrong; I was the savior and they needed me. I never once thought that I needed myself, and more than anything else, I needed to be my own hero. It took me well into my thirties to come to this mindset.

I needed to walk each step; I needed that codependent family relationship, one that I was forever proud of and to an extent, still

*woven*

am today. I needed to be burned, hurt, and scarred emotionally. Of course, I did not have this foresight as I experienced it all. I was miserable, lost, misguided. But today, I know for certain like every step you take to get to the top of a mountain, it all needed to take form in the manner that it did.

Still not knowing who I was or what I stood for in my late teens, I affixed myself to the fairy tale of "and they lived *happily ever after*." I met someone who changed my life forever; some may argue for the worse, but I've reframed the narrative to believe it was for the absolute best.

He was different. He was kind, patient, gentle, funny, and caring. We had so much fun together and spent every possible moment with each other. If we weren't in class individually, we were side by side. It was beautiful and so different than any other relationship I had ever experienced. Mentally and emotionally, it was love. It was what Hollywood movies were made of and the kind of love Céline Dion sings about (can you tell I'm Canadian?!). I thought I had found my soul mate, the piece to complete my puzzle.

What I didn't recognize was the love bombing, the slow, steady, intentional manipulation and control. I was blinded with love to the fact that I affixed my codependency from my parents and projected it onto this individual, creating a family away from my physical family. At the time, I truly felt the attention and devotion was a symbol of true love. I thought I was finally being accepted for who I was (really, not even knowing myself who I was). Early on in what would be a ten-year relationship, I was introduced to his family, and he was introduced to mine. It was the first time I ever "brought anyone home." We were in what I thought at the time to be a mature and serious relationship. I knew in my heart and soul that he would be the person with whom I would grow old.

The irony, however, was that it wasn't always sparkles and rainbows. It wasn't perfect or even comfortable all the time. But I was logical. I would remind myself that no relationship is perfect; each love story looks and feels different, and this one was simply mine. I continued to brush aside my gut instinct and overlooked comments and questions by friends and family. I continued to excuse behavior and weigh the good against the bad. I knew what I was experiencing wasn't "right" or healthy, by any means. I knew if it were happening to a friend or family member, I would instantly tell them to pack their bags and get out of the situation. I just couldn't do it for myself. I was in too deep. Our lives were too enmeshed and entangled. *What would people say? What would my parents think? What would society think of my family?* The generation-old sociocultural jingle echoed in my mind like affirmations on repeat. Much like my past relationships and experiences, I was addicted to the attention; something in the most twisted way possible was magnetic. I continued to be magnetized toward him, us, our relationship, and all that it meant.

*woven*

And so, I stayed. I lived in silence as the person I had hoped to be one day slowly disappeared. "There wasn't explicit abuse . . . " I would convince myself. I was never hit, and there was no yelling or arguing. But there were deep, harsh words from time to time, and there was endless isolation and silence. I questioned every move I made and every word I uttered. I no longer recognized the woman I'd become. Looking in the mirror, I'd see the shell of a woman I used to be. I continued to hear that jingle . . . *How could I end it now? How could I just walk away? Where would I go? Who would want me? What would people say?*

Everything changed, however, when my beautiful, vivacious, and sassy little boss babe, Natalie, was born. I never saw myself as strong enough or worthy enough for more until I gave birth. Now I had something, *someone* really to live for—someone for whom I desired more and for whom to be my best self every day. I'd be a fool to say it was all for me (it wasn't), and it often isn't. Everything I am today, and the reason I'm able to be at peace with my past is because it was all worth it for HER. The meekness stops with me. The chase for external validation stops with me. She will be empowered to be her own woman from day one, and she is. She will live her life, make her mistakes, and no longer wear the cape of societal and cultural expectations the way I did. The chase for perfectionism ends with me. We, as a powerful mom and daughter duo, are after global domination, of our voice, our Self. We shine our quirks, strengths, and everything that makes us who we are with pride and grace.

As I stand before the world in my almost mid-thirties, no longer fully that meek, quiet, embarrassed person described in this chapter, I feel at peace with my life journey. So, how did I get here? Because I chose Her and myself. Because life is too short to live under the weight of gender norms, cultural norms, and any societal norms that are forced upon us as women, as humans. Because at our core, whatever you identify as, no matter where you come from, no matter what your life looks like, you have a voice that needs to be heard, a soul that deserves to be honored, and an essence that desires to be cherished and respected. And I'll be damned if I don't change the generational dialogue for myself and the rest of my lineage. Today, I am confident, bold, and outspoken. Today, I take charge of my life, live life on my own terms, march to the beat of my heart, and take control of my life, on my own. And it is an exercise in self-awareness, self-love, and conscious living. So, how did I get to today? The answer is extremely loaded. I needed to be broken to make myself whole again. The threads that wove me together needed to come undone and be torn apart into shreds so I could weave a whole pattern, create a whole new design for my life, and be the boss of my life—bolder, stronger, softer, and more open than ever. Today, because of every single second of my life—a past that I hold on to and a present that I am carving—I'm the mom I longed to be. I'm the woman I always saw as untouchable and indestructible. I am whole because time and time again, I was broken and walked through a fire that I never thought I would or could walk through. And you, my friend, can too!

*Section 2*

# ROOT TO RISE

SARA COSTA

PATRICIA MORGAN

KIM SORICHETTI

SONALI THAKER

LEANNE FORD

LISA TOWN

I remember, I remember, I remember all those moments when I was supposed to play into what was expected of me, what was charted out for me by others.

Where their words dictated what would become of me if I let them . . .

*"You'll never amount to anything . . . you're much like your mother."*

*"You don't have a nice voice. You can't sing."*

*"I don't want you. You look just like your father."*

*"I don't want you. You look just like your mother."*

*"You're cold, just like your father."*

*"You're emotional, just like your mother."*

*"You're too outspoken. You'll never find a man. Next time, try making him feel good. He needs to feel important, not you."*

*woven*

*"You'll never finish high school, let alone go to university."*

*"Perhaps you shouldn't be in university . . . given your background and circumstances, it might be better if you went to college or took a year off."*

*"You'll never be a writer. You're not good at it."*

*"Your Arts degree is useless. You cannot make a living with it."*

*"You cannot be outspoken in the workplace. You have to bite your tongue. You have to tolerate their shit to get bills paid."*

*"Your needs don't matter. Do you think you are the only woman to have given birth, have a hard birth, experienced postpartum depression, worked nights, and built a business? Get over yourself. Others have done it, not talked about it, and now they have multiple kids."*

*"You're worthless, why don't you go die? You're a burden. You're of no use when you don't bring the income you used to."*

*"You're a one-child wonder. That's your claim to fame. You're not really a mother. You only have one child."*

*"These things happen, you just have to compromise. Marriage isn't easy. Why don't you distract yourself with something else?"*

*"You're not meant to be an entrepreneur. Why is it taking you so long?"*

*"You're irresponsible, selfish, lazy. You chose to leave your job. Only selfish people pursue their passion. Life doesn't work that way."*

*"Your own parents didn't want you, so they married you off to someone else."*

*"Why isn't a regular life enough for you?"*

I remember all the moments when these words hit my soul, deep and sharp, turning into a dull ache that just sits there year after year, countless courses, mentors, and self-help books gone by. Heck, some days I still wrestle with these demons inside my head and out. And I remind myself of who I am, what I came here to do. My soul contract that God and the Universe entrusted me with.

I remember during the deepest, darkest moments of my life how it felt to hear these words repeated over and over again, like a loop that won't stop unless I consciously choose to release these words and the stories they hold. Until I realized that I am always loved and supported by God, by the Universe. That when you release expectations of yourself and others, their words will wash off your back. It might sting, but you'll be able to use those stings as fuel to help you propel further. Momentarily, those words and the emotional imprint they carry might make you feel like you're being uprooted. And perhaps you are in many ways. Perhaps you're being asked to stay rooted in your power and rise above all the storm clouds that come your way.

So, I ask you this . . .

Can you let go of all expectations and see beyond what is present in front of you? Can you trust that you are held and supported even when it doesn't feel like it? Especially when it doesn't feel like it?

Can you trust that your soul knows languages of lifetimes and eons and it is here for a purpose?

Can you trust that you are to bloom where you are planted for that is exactly the soil that will build you up? Can you trust that you are always being led in every moment and every interaction and every fall and in every climb?

Can you trust that your language is powerful, it shapes your life, and it is the cornerstone of your personal power?

You see, your body, mind, and soul don't understand anything else but energetic vibrations and soul frequencies—you are whole just as you are. You need not constrict your expansion for anyone else. Take up space, boldly and wildly. Allow yourself to fall into the pleasures that call your name. They are yours for a reason. Claim them and stand in your strength, your divinity, your power, and attract. Show me. Lead me, call me. Guide me. Empower me to go first. Always. Even when the vision feels a bit hazy, but the vibes feel so clear as day. And so it is. And so it is. And so it is.

# Bloom

Bloom where you're planted.

Finding meaning and blessing through every moment.

Opportunity in every setback.

Own your story.

Own your choices.

Own your becoming.

Get bare naked with your soul.


Every time you're faced with an unknown, simply breathe.

Hand over heart.

Quell the noises you hear inside and out.

Remind yourself that you've seen this before.

It looks different.

It might feel different.

But this, this space, you've been here before.

In many moons and lifetimes.

You've overcome much worse.

All that matters is who you are now.

How you're coming into full bloom.

Honor your becoming.

Only you need to feel it and see it.

*woven*

# Chapter 5

# What If Someone Tells You No . . .

Sara Costa

*Sara Costa*

Sara Costa was born in Toronto, Ontario, on May 9, 1995. Sara is twenty-six years

of age and identifies as a positive individual. She studied early childhood education

and pursued her dream of becoming a teacher. She is a sister and a daughter. She

values time with her family and friends very much, whether playing board games or

going for long nature walks. Sara gained a passion for traveling, and she works at

the airport where she enjoys meeting new people and being immersed in different

cultures. Her motto in life is to be happy, smile often, and do anything and everything

you dream of! If you were to die tomorrow, would you be happy? That's the question

she continuously asks herself and that pushes her to get out of her comfort zone!

:camera: @sarratravels

To my family and friends, I dedicate this chapter to you. Thank you my mom, dad, sister, and boyfriend for uplifting me and believing in me. You allowed me to pursue my dream and accomplish any dream I had. To everyone else who has been along for the ride, you know who you are. Remember that without you and your positivity and encouragement, I wouldn't be here. Always chase whatever dream you have, even if they say no.

"Don't ever let anyone tell you who you are or what you can or cannot do. That power is yours alone. A power that is shaped by the cards you've been dealt and the experiences you've had. A power that is woven with the blood, sweat, and tears of your ancestors. You are the change you've been waiting for."

# What If Someone Tells You No . . .

*Each time a woman stands up for herself, without knowing it possibly, without claiming it, she stands up for all women.*
–Maya Angelou

Women's empowerment is a critical movement that I believe everyone should support. It might seem like we have been at it for decades and it no longer needs to be a pivotal movement world over, yet here we are—persisting for the right to choose ourselves, our bodies, our voice, our autonomy, our identity. As unbelievable as it seems, women all over the world still have to fight to be seen, heard, and feel safe in their bodies, their environment, their homes, their workplaces, and more. They have to fight arduously to receive their own identity and freedom. Sad, right? That is why I have fought this battle, and it has led me to where I am today. I took this quote by Coco Chanel to heart: "*A girl should be two things: Who she wants and what she wants."* You could say that it's the thread that continues to weave together my life story. Here goes . . .

My story started back in grade two. Yes, you read that correctly. Grade two. I started at a new school, and I was the "new girl" in the class, which excited me until . . . I had no hope of surviving. I spoke limited English, as my first language is Portuguese, even though I was born in Canada. My parents were both born in Portugal. They moved to Canada in their early twenties in pursuit of a better life and opportunity for them and the generations that would follow, which, in this case, hi! Times were hard in Portugal at the time. My mom's dream was to be a teacher, and my dad always wanted to start his own business. As it always does, life happens, and you know what that means: My sister was born, and five years later, I came here earthside as well. My parents then purchased their first house. Those dreams of becoming a teacher were distant memories for my mother, desires that were now locked away for safekeeping because that's just how life goes. My mother has now worked at the same factory for over thirty years. As for my dad, he has built his own business as a landscaper.

Nevertheless, I am extremely proud of both parents because they have been able to provide a life for my sister and me that I had never dreamed of. But that pride in my parents is always accompanied with a twinge of bittersweet sadness, a shadow if you will. The shadow of sacrifice, expectations, what it means for both my sister and me to fulfill our respective dreams and make our parents proud of us, to give meaning to their sacrifice because they basically suffered for us to live. I remember my mom walking to the bus stop with twenty-five centimeters of snow on the ground while carrying me and holding my sister's hand. As for my dad, he can easily put in fifteen-hour days to ensure we have food on the table. Today, my sister is an early childhood educator and en route to becoming a teacher while taking care of her two little girls and working full time, and her husband is a frontline worker in a hospital, working countless hours as well. The sacrifices our generations past have made is never lost on us. You could say it is one of the reasons why we strive to achieve whatever it is we have our hearts set on. We didn't get to this "pedestal" of success as defined by us on our own. We have had a massive support system helping us through the thick and thin of it all, including my partner, his family, my friends, and my relatives, all for whom I am so thankful.

Why does any of this matter? **Because people will tell you who you are supposed to be, what you can do, and what you cannot do, if you let them.** My fate would have been sealed in grade two since I spoke limited English at the time. Like every child, I was excited to have made two new friends. I was excited to simply be there with kids my own age. However, as soon as I entered that classroom, my teacher had a plan for me. I wish I could say it was a good one. She advised me that I had to go into an English as a Second Language (ESL) classroom, and at the time, that meant being excluded from the rest of the students in my class. Educational environments weren't as inclusive back then as they are today, and still, there is so much work to be done. Today, students are integrated into the classroom if they need additional support (which is fantastic!), and they learn in an environment that is inclusive. In all honesty, did I need the additional assistance from my ESL classes? Absolutely! Did I, as a seven-year-old child, need to hear someone in a position of authority whisper, "Sara doesn't have the capacity to stay within a classroom setting" to my ESL teacher? Absolutely not. Granted, I couldn't speak the language well, but I could still listen and comprehend English effectively. My heart sank upon hearing those words. It tore my spirit. Nothing dampens the enthusiasm of a school-aged kid like telling them they aren't cut out for the same things as their peers or making them feel like they are less than their peers. So, what do you do? What do you say? **You get back up and you ensure you become as successful as humanly possible.**

I began working young. Working hard, being persistent, and persevering no matter what were values that were instilled in me from a young age. I saw my parents work tirelessly, all so my sister and I could have the life and opportunities they envisioned

*woven*

for us. They never quit when things got hard. Instead, they would buckle down and keep going. So, naturally, I followed suit. At five years of age, I helped clean at my mom's work. I watered the plants and pretended I was typing on their 1980's keyboards. And here we are, twenty years later, and I still help clean every Friday or Saturday, except now I wipe down desks, vacuum, and pick up things off the floor. Sounds glamorous, right? I worked part time at a kids' store for about twenty-two hours each week, all while completing high school full time. Everyone thought I was crazy, but again, my mindset was always, "I am going somewhere . . . I've got places to go . . . and that somewhere will reach the top."

Working at the kids' store allowed me to meet many unique individuals, yet there I was, seventeen years old and still thirsting for adventure, growth, and, of course, the next step on the ladder of success. The next adventure was crazy all right. I was scrolling through indeed.com because I needed a big-girl job. I cannot help but chuckle when I think of that moment when I was on the hunt for a "big-girl job," but that's what happens when you have a point to prove, a need to prove to yourself that you're good enough, worthy enough, smart enough, pretty enough, desirable enough. I applied to an airline, and as soon as I hit Send, this thought surfaced: *Hmm, they won't even call me.* Guess what? Three weeks later, I received a call. It was April 15, and I will never forget that date. I was invited to come in for an interview. Everything moved fast as it always does. I was starting college and working full-time hours at the airport. At the time, I was the youngest airline employee. I was working and attending school full time (I don't recommend this schedule to anyone). It was extremely stressful, and I ended up in the hospital for two weeks. My lesson? Don't overwork yourself to the detriment of your well-being while pursuing your version of success.

Looking back, I can now say that working at the airline is what afforded me the privilege of traveling the world with my parents, my sister, my friends, and my boyfriend. And I emphasize my parents because we were never fortunate enough to travel when I was younger. I heard my classmates say things like "I am off to Florida" or "I am going to see my grandparents around the world," but the income my parents earned only extended so far. We never went without, and we were well provided for and cared for; however, some money for leisure time as a family would have been the cherry on top of the icing of a life that was built upon hard work, love, and sacrifice. At the airline, I became a brand ambassador and was featured in many magazines, newspapers, and even on a commercial. I was also chosen as a temporary manager, which taught me a lot about problem solving, networking, and engagement.

I can go on and on about my work experience because the opportunities kept appearing—camp counselor, respite care for a children's center, landscaping with my father, home stager, and client relations with a construction company. And I continued to seize these opportunities, pursue them, and carpe diem the heck out of my life, professionally and personally. This thirst for adventure, paired with a passion to make a difference, do meaningful work, and be the best I can be no matter what I do and where I go, is what led me to pursue a second degree as a qualified teacher in Ontario. One of my proudest moments was purchasing my own condo in downtown Toronto. These may seem like material markers of success, but beneath that pinnacle lies grit, persistence, and tons of trial and error, as well as following my passions, always seeking growth, putting myself in opportunities and places where I could continue learning, and, of course, a rock-solid foundation of a work ethic and growth mindset.

As I continue my growth and evolution, it is my desire and goal to give back to my parents who have worked so hard to provide me with what I have today and to inspire the ones around me and the future generation. Success wasn't given to me, it was earned. It was earned through the countless sleepless nights and through the cries, the pleas for help, and most important, sheer persistence. If there is one thing you take away from reading my story, may it be this: Never give up on your dream. It doesn't matter how old you are, where you come from, and what your story brings. You hold the power and the key to changing how your story ends.

You hold the key to your success. Don't ever let anyone tell you who you are or what you can or cannot do. That power is yours alone. A power that is shaped by the cards you've been dealt and the experiences you've had. A power that is woven with the blood, sweat, and tears of your ancestors. You are the change you've been waiting for. You have the power to change the trajectory of your life and the lives of those who come after you. It all starts with you.

*woven*

# Chapter 6

# Identity Behind the Illness

Patricia Morgan

*Patricia Morgan*

Patricia Morgan is a sweet-natured, animal-loving wife and mother. She lives in the quiet town of Paris, Ontario, just an hour outside of Toronto, with her husband, Jason, two little boys, Nathan (3) and Bennett (1), and their dog, Ellie.

Growing up, Patricia wanted nothing more than to be a mom. While her path to motherhood was a bumpy one due to health and fertility issues, she has overcome those obstacles and loves nothing more than spending time with her little family and watching the budding friendship between her boys. Patricia lives with a chronic illness called Ehlers Danlos Syndrome (EDS), which has forcefully dictated much of the way she has lived over the past fifteen years. In the early years, she did all she could to hide the reality of her illness from those beyond her most inner circle, but more recently, she has recognized and embraced the positive impact that she can have by sharing her story. On her Instagram page, she shares information to educate and raise awareness about what EDS is, and she provides a window into the struggles in her life so that others living with chronic illness can see that they are not alone. More than anything else, Patricia wants to ensure those struggling always remember that their diagnosis does not define who they are.

 @edswarriormom

For my husband: I do not know how I got so lucky to find you at seventeen. There is no way I can put into words how grateful I am for you. For Nathan and Bennett, my sweet miracles: You bring more love and laughter into my life than I thought possible. To everyone with an invisible illness, may you know that you are never alone in your struggle.

"*Gratitude* simply means recognizing and appreciating what you have rather than focusing on what you do not."

# Identity Behind the Illness

*We read to know we are not alone.*
-C. S. Lewis

*How can I go on like this? It hurts so much. How can anyone live a life filled with chronic pain?*

These are the thoughts that float through my mind on a daily basis. The only time I don't feel pain is when I am sleeping. There are days where I loathe myself and what it feels like to be within this body marred with chronic illness and pain. Days where I can't get out of bed and need to ask my husband to stay home to help me with the kids even though I know that he is already stressed at work. Days when I feel, at best, like a part-time mother because the pain can be so severe that I need to rest most of the day. Days when I have to cancel my plans with a friend at the last minute, yet again, because even though I mentally and emotionally need companionship, my pain will not give me a break. In fact, my pain renders me inconsistent, flaky, and sometimes nonexistent. I hate that I have very little control over myself and my really bad days. It is really hard when you go to bed with a plan for the next day but wake up unable to follow through on it. It is even harder going to bed with that plan and knowing that you are likely going to wake up feeling like you've let down yourself or someone you care about.

There are many days when I barely get to spend time with my husband, let alone have any form of intimacy. By the end of the day, the pain is too much to even consider any output of energy. When we do get any time together, it is hard to fully enjoy it; it is like a tug-of-war between the pleasure it brings to be together and the pain it causes, whether we are just staying up to watch a show or participating in anything more. It makes us feel like passing ships each day, and I feel guilty and wish I could be a better wife.

We spend more money than we would like to on takeout food because I rarely have the energy to make dinner. We eat peanut butter and jelly or Kraft dinner more often than I would like to admit because there just never seems to be enough time in the day to get the rest and sleep that I need in order to plan, grocery shop, prep, cook, and clean up.

My husband and I want to make the most out of our life with our kids. I'm the happiest making memories with them, but my husband and I pay for those memories dearly—me with the pain and subsequent symptoms being so unbearable from pushing myself that I am unable to get out of bed, and him for then needing to take care of the boys as well as me. While those memories are a lifeline, something for me to look back on and remind myself of the happy days during bad ones, it also causes such guilt that I just can't be normal and that I pay for everything I do. Whether it's going to a family gathering or going out with friends or even something as small as going to the park, my pain increases as do all my symptoms.

While I am asking you to imagine these scenarios, I would not wish anyone to have to actually face them the way that I do.

I do not share this information because I want your help, your pity, or your sympathy. I share it because it is important to understand my journey to understand my message. If you have a chronic illness, I hope by reading my chapter, you know that you are not alone and that your illness does not define you. If you don't have a chronic illness, I hope in reading my chapter that you gain a greater understanding of our struggle, which will then help you create a safe cocoon for anyone else who may be navigating the entanglement of chronic illness for the rest of their life.

For a long time, I was private about my life. I didn't want to open up to anyone for fear of being misunderstood and judged. From an early age, I would use writing as a tool instead to vent when I felt I couldn't speak, to gather my thoughts, or to cope when I was going through a hard time. For me, it was easier to be vulnerable on the page than to a person. Writing has always been a part of my life, but it wasn't until I experienced many years of struggle with major health issues that I wondered if I could use my story for more. We all have a story to tell, one that is unique to us but that has the ability to connect to many, and we just have to believe that it is a story worth telling.

Before being diagnosed with EDS, I was just a kid growing up, the youngest of four girls, who always dreamed of being a mom. I loved animals and wanted to be a veterinarian. My husband jokes that in another life I would be the girl from the show *Heartland*, living on a ranch with horses and dogs and raising a family.

My earliest memory of living with headaches was when I was ten years old and at Disney World with my family. I remember lying in the hotel room because my head hurt so much. My headaches would come and go, which led to a CT scan that came back "normal." With no better explanation, my headaches were chalked up to the presence of mold at my school and nothing more. Years later, my headaches were still there, off and on, and I often got sick, sometimes even having to miss school and do extra work at home to make up for it, but nothing was really made of it, and we did not know that we would need to dig deeper. It was just who I was until I was eighteen. I was living on campus at Brock

University and attending my first year of classes. I lived with headaches coming and going, usually a few times each week, but one day in early 2007, they changed and affected me all day, every day. I remember spending a week in bed because I thought I was just having a really bad migraine that would eventually go away. Sadly, that was not the case, and so began my journey for answers.

For the last fifteen years, I've been in the passenger seat of the car that is my life, and I've helplessly watched as my invisible illness has taken the wheel. I ended up leaving school because I couldn't concentrate with the pain I was in. My vision became blurry, and I'd be nauseated and so tired from being in pain that it was impossible to keep up with classes. By the end of that year, I found myself bedbound and needing help to walk because, along with my head pain, my scoliosis curve had gotten so severe that I needed surgery. I was hoping that my head pain was caused by my back issues, and that hope was growing by the day leading up to May 2008 when I underwent spinal surgery. The recovery was challenging, and I remember walking up the stairs on my own for the first time . . . it had been months since I had done that alone, and it felt surreal. It left me feeling that I ought to never take for granted the simple daily tasks that not everyone can do so simply.

Unfortunately, after the recovery and healing from surgery was done, the constant pain in my head was still alive and well. I spent years going from doctor to doctor, trying to figure out what was wrong with me. I remember in the early days, one of my doctors told me that I "just needed to push through it." I left that appointment in tears. I thought, *I'm in so much pain; why doesn't he believe me?* I moved from specialist to specialist and eventually ended up at a headache and pain specialist. He was a great doctor who wanted to help me and believed in what I was feeling. From that point on, it was trial and error, working with many different types of medication to find the right fit, the right dosage. I tried every medication and injection with none of the relief and all the negative side effects. I left every appointment feeling so hopeless and defeated. *How was I a person that modern medicine couldn't help? Why couldn't anyone find out what was wrong with me?* For anyone who is at this spot in their health journey, you know how frustrating and hopeless not having answers can be. You cannot be blamed for wondering if you'll be living with this struggle for the rest of your life and never really understanding why.

By 2011 I had to leave my job. Why? Because chronic illness that isn't always visible renders you inconsistent and unreliable in the current society we live in. I've not worked since, and my situation does not seem likely to change any time soon. In a world where most people define themselves (at least in part) by what they do, it's a terrible feeling to not have that part of my identity. In 2013 I found my way to a geneticist because of an Ehlers Danlos Syndrome diagnosis in the family. I went into that appointment thinking I would rule out EDS because, at that time, I didn't believe I had the normal symptoms of an EDS patient. Little did I know that EDS presents itself in various ways. The geneticist confirmed my diagnosis, and we finally had an answer for all my symptoms. The same diagnosis has been confirmed on numerous occasions since, the most recent in 2019, as the criteria for EDS had recently changed. Every single time they run these tests, I get my hopes up that I will be told I don't have it but rather have something else with more successful treatment options.

Ehlers Danlos Syndrome is a connective tissue disorder. We have connective tissue throughout our entire body, so EDS can cause a wide variety of debilitating symptoms. Not only does it affect our joints, causing dislocations/subluxation and pain, but it can also cause gastrointestinal problems, fatigue, chronic pain, migraines or extreme head pain, vision problems and postural tachycardia syndrome (POTS), to name a few of the many manifestations. For me, my most debilitating symptom is the constant severe pain in my head. I also have POTS, which can cause its own debilitating symptoms and a wide variety of other problems, but the chronic pain in my head has been the constant that changed my life.

Ehlers Danlos Syndrome does not have a cure, so it's difficult knowing that nothing is going to help me get better. It has taken me a long time to accept this fate, and there are still times when my symptoms get worse, and I pray something fixable shows up on a

CT scan or MRI that could change the outlook for my health. It is very heavy to think that, at such a young age, I already know I will live the rest of my life in pain. When you are searching for so many years for a diagnosis, it is because you are also searching for a cure—anything that will take the pain away, make you feel better, and let you live a normal life. So, even though having a diagnosis is wonderful because doctors now take my symptoms seriously, it's hard not to wish that I was still searching for an answer to explain my suffering. Ehlers Danlos and its comorbidities define a huge part of my life, a reality that will never change.

After coming to terms with what my health would look like in the future, my psychologist helped me understand that I had to regularly remind myself that my whole life did not need to be defined by EDS. I had to take my life back. I had to pick myself up, dust myself off, and just keep swimming. I decided that though my circumstances won't change, my perspective on life sure could. Ehlers Danlos dictates so many aspects of my day-to-day life, but I am unwilling to let it make me feel powerless. Examining my life with a focus on what I have to be thankful for has shown me that beyond my diagnosis and health struggles, there is so much more that defines me. For instance, ever since I was a child, I dreamed of being a mother. Today, against what feels like all odds, I am a mother to two handsome little boys. In the process of trying to start a family, Jason and I struggled with infertility, we had a

*woven*

miscarriage, and ultimately, both of our boys came to us via IVF. There is no better proof in my life that no matter the obstacles put in my path, I won't let my diagnosis keep me from fulfilling the dreams that I have. I have the family that I had always dreamed of: I have a loving and caring husband who has been by my side since I was seventeen and when all my pain really started taking over. I have my eldest son, Nathan, who is a sweet, funny, and loving little boy as well as a great big brother, and I have my youngest son, Bennett, who lights up when he sees me and never lets me forget how loved and needed I am. It is these moments that bring me back to gratitude, surrender, and loving self-acceptance.

Gratitude does not mean pretending that you won't be faced with challenges, heartbreak, or tragedy. It does not mean seeing the world through rose-colored glasses, nor does it mean pretending to be happy in the face of pain and adversity. Gratitude simply means recognizing and appreciating what you have rather than focusing on what you do not. I know that our lives, as people with chronic illnesses, may look very different than we ever imagined, but by focusing on being grateful, we can magnify the good in our lives, which will hopefully minimize the focus on the bad. There are many days I wish I could be the mom and wife I always envisioned in my mind that I would be, one without any chronic illness whatsoever. That life is not my reality, and I choose to be grateful that "mom" and "wife" are my titles. That I am loved no matter what my day looks like—no matter what I am able or unable to do. That my worth as a human being isn't defined by my chronic illness, not anymore at least. My husband and boys are my reason for living, and I truly do not think I would be here today without them.

It might sound clichéd, but we all have a reason for being and a reason for living, and if you feel like you don't, I invite you to focus on all that is good within your life and the lessons that you can take from all of the challenges. Pain is unbearable; it drains you and makes you fight not only a physical battle, but a mental one as well. What years of counseling have taught me is that gratitude will be the antidote that helps you navigate your pain. Happiness is in the little things: a friend stopping by for a conversation, a hug from a parent or sibling, a dog who always knows when it's a really bad day, or a partner or child saying, "I love you."

I remind myself every single day that I am still me, Patricia Morgan! A daughter, a sister, an aunt, a friend, and, most importantly, a wife and mother. I am a lover of animals and want to volunteer at an animal shelter when my boys are older. I love yoga and the mind, body, and soul connection I have during practice. I love writing, and here I am, writing this chapter, and I've already been published in a digital magazine. It feels therapeutic to write my thoughts and feelings on paper. I know that my words and my story will help others who are experiencing something similar.

*woven*

These desires, these dreams, these goals are all me. I am still ME. I am not my diagnosis, which is a lesson I am constantly learning and reminding myself of every day.

As I write this chapter, I am experiencing one of the worst flare-ups I've had in a long time. But here I am, pushing through and pursuing my dream of becoming an author, one word at a time. To me, every time I write even a single word, it shows me that I have the strength to fight through the battle that my illness puts at my feet and the persistence to come out the other side in pursuit of my hopes and dreams.

My life is made up of a series of trade-offs: If I do this, I might not be able to do that. If I make dinner, I probably won't be able to go to the park with my kids. I regularly shower at night because it's exhausting and needs to be followed by sleep. If I spend a full day outside of my house with family or friends, I will need a few days to spend in bed recovering. I plan out each week, and there are still days beyond my control. The fact that I have to make these choices could easily lead to feelings of depression, and I am not going to pretend like they never do, but I do all that I can to choose to have a positive mindset and to be grateful for all that I have, some of which (including having my children) I never thought I would. There is no doubt that life with chronic illness is hard, but we are all showing everyone, especially our kids, just how strong we are by persevering through that struggle, all while maintaining an attitude of gratitude. We are teaching them that they, too, can develop the resilience and strength to push through anything. Your mindset, whether you have a chronic illness or not, can change how you make it through each day. For some, just pushing yourself to get up and get dressed is a huge step in the right direction. Be gentle with yourself in each moment. Move through each day being conscious of how many spoons you have to work with while being grateful for what those spoons allowed you to accomplish. (If you suffer from a chronic illness and are not familiar with Christine Miserandino's "The Spoon Theory," I highly recommend reading it, as it does a great job of explaining the limited capacity that many of us have.) It might be at a different rate than you imagined before being diagnosed, but here you are, still forging on and embracing each day and what it has to offer, making the most of the one life you're here to live, making everyone who knows you proud. You are more than just your diagnosis, you can still achieve your dreams, and you can be happy and love life. Life may look different than what you thought it would, and living with your illness is likely the hardest thing you are doing day in and day out, but one thing my amazing online community of warriors has taught me is that we are all in this together, and together we've got this.

*woven*

# *Chapter 7*

# Embracing You

KIM SORICHETTI

Kim Sorichetti

Kim Sorichetti is the wearer of countless hats. She is a mother of three remarkable teenage humans (two boys and one girl), she is the wife to an enthusiastic man who is her shield and love, and she is a person of creativity, soul, and triumph. Kim was an integral part of the corporate world, spending most of her career in telecommunications, and she has upheld an entrepreneurial spirit since she can remember. Today, she is the owner of two flourishing businesses: she is a consultant in the telecommunications industry and she runs her "baby," KasaDesign, a real estate staging and design firm specializing in home and commercial staging. Her passion for interior design and real estate came into full force in 2002 after her first son was born. While she enjoyed being a stay-at-home mom, she was compelled to pursue her musing full time.

As the blueprint to her personal life evolved, she never looked back at the corporate world, and she continues to focus her journey on entrepreneurship. Kim's business statement holds true that everyone deserves a beautiful space in home, heart, and mind. Her sentiment is often exposed on her sleeve, and her desire to support others who support themselves is prominent. As she ventured into residential move number twenty of her lifetime, the whispers to tell her story were spoken, her purpose discovered, and her story shared. "I will be happy when ... " was her virtuous beginning.

⊙ @kasadesigninc

My dear children, the journey of motherhood is heartwarmingly fulfilling. As a child, you learn so much from your parents, and as a parent, you learn so much from your children. There isn't a book that teaches you how to do life the "right" way or what your purpose is, but more so the ability to have a connection to yourself and those you love. Inner peace, happiness, self-love and the growth toward self-worth creates the unmistaken ability to enjoy life's moments. To my husband and soul mate, as we drift through the peaks and valleys of our journey, we continue to learn balance as we devote as much space to the climb as we do to appreciating the landscapes. To my family and amazing sisters who are only ever one call away, you are always loved as are my sisterhood friends, Rachel, Kathy, Colleen, Carolyn, Paula, Cheryl, Anna, and Diane. You are all the reason I smile today.

"*Practicing* omitting the phrase 'I will be happy when . . .' is a virtuous place to start."

# Embracing You

*Love yourself first and everything else falls into line. You really have to love yourself to get anything done in this world.*
–Lucille Ball

As I sit in my office and stare out the window, I see life being rebirthed all around me—the trees budding with spring foliage, the squirrels scurrying about in the forest, the birds chirping in the background—I am reminded that my existence is all mine. The colorful life that was a promise from childhood can only be navigated by me. Like the paint on the walls can be altered, the creakiness of the floors can be replaced, and the cottage-like kitchen can be shaped into a dwelling where we will revel as a family, to laugh, to share, to experience and create memories. **It is time to step out of the unfinished interior of my house into the live exterior world of aspiration and continue my journey of personal healing.**

Sharing my story is a dominant part in what has brought me to understanding the feelings of loneliness and negative self-worth that have been suffocating me for decades. It is easy to carry myself with the grand smile, the shielding shell, and the positive image, but deep down inside there has been hurt and heaviness that needs to be spoken. Learning how to expose the vulnerability with my husband / soul mate has really been a work in progress, a new type of unfurling, a new unlearning of everything that once was, so we can grow together anew. He has a new understanding for why I am who I am. Peace, love, happiness, and success have become my narrative.

It has taken me to the age of fifty to reflect on my dysfunctional childhood and the heaviness of the wounds in my heart and on my shoulders that have long held me back from loving myself enough to believe I am worthy of anything and everything. My journey wasn't exactly how it was planned to be in my fairy tale, but more like the exit to get away. The nineteen residential moves from childhood to today as I step into move number twenty have given me permission to stop running from myself. Like the "world card," number twenty is symbolic of "judgment." A time when we can practice internal reflection and reinstate an empathetic understanding about our presence and what we need to do to foster as humans. And I believe I am there. Looking inward, I now realize that I spent much of my life in escapism, fronting what is

*woven*

now known to me as self-love and self-worth. I spent years hiding from my hurt, my wounds, when all along what they and I needed was fresh air to breathe and heal.

Buried in the roots of my soul are the wounds that have been carried for years as the oldest of four siblings. I was so young and instantly thrust into taking responsibility for my three younger siblings. It was survival and protection from the household eruptions of toxic arguments, alcohol, and tensions. Those traits have traveled life's road with me and now I am prepared to release them and leave them behind in the next half of my life, which I have deemed to be filled with peace, love, happiness, and success . . . because I am worthy.

As a woman in my twenties, I asked my mother, "What is my purpose?" I remember her answer so clearly: "To enjoy life and be loved by those around you." Honestly, I am embarrassed to say I am not sure I have ever felt truly loved or felt truly taken care of. I have doubt I have ever experienced the feeling of being worthy. My journey has been independent, solo, and structured. The healing process has come with maturity and embracing positive thought, surrounding myself with those who add value and happiness to my daily life and getting rid of those who do not. No longer marginalizing my values and the feelings of being judged by others but knowing that my universal space is part of something so much bigger.

As the mother of three humans, my purpose is to change the pattern and cultivate a life in which they feel so worthy and loved. The blueprint for change will be reshaped with energetic design so at the age of fifty, they are not hopelessly running but rather reflecting on a journey filled with happiness, fearlessness, positivity, and strength, never having to suppress their inner voice to live a life of self-worthiness and love. Each of us have different callings, but when you hear the soft voice to share your story, there is a reason and purpose.

Starting the healing journey came with tears and laughs, simplicity and struggles, awakenings and rest. Admittedly, I have been lost—lost in my soul—with the ability to give the persona that the exterior face is fine and full of joy and smiles. It is easier to carry on the daily routine in survival mode, filled with taking care of others, giving, sharing, and caring, all the while missing out on giving that same to ourselves. Certainly, successful in career, parenthood, and nurturing friendships, but barely nurturing and nourishing myself and my soul. Barely having any personal boundaries and accepting exploitation as love and kinship. Now, that cross is destined to rest. At peace. It was in a moment of self-reflection when the overwhelming realization dawned on me that I am a stranger to myself in my own home. I knew what to do for others and how to treat others, but I never offered the same reverence and equal merit to myself. With consideration to peace, happiness, self-worth, love,

*woven*

and success, combined with the knowledge that a quick fix was not the answer, it was a struggle to cultivate a spiritual calm in my mind. I had to let go of judgments from others or people who might influence my thoughts and border myself with powerful and positive forces.

## Inner Peace

Born as a type A personality and having two boys following the same, in 2002 and 2005, I was gifted a sweet little girl in 2006. She is calm, happy, confident, and humble. My daughter was truly put in my world to teach me to appreciate the little things that are important, to stop and smell the flowers, and to slow down and enjoy life. To take instances one step at a time, to be enduring, to make the greatest of all moments, and to forget about mindless flashes until the next day. The pandemic has granted time to reflect on past years and then take a step back to discover what is important and touches upright in my soul. Spending time in solitude, taking in my surroundings, I started reveling in the simple pleasures. For the first time in a long time, I started to ask myself questions like "Do you want to sit on a bench today or walk on a trail?" These questions, though basic and mundane, held a magic within them. The magic of healing, the magic of cultivating inner peace, of being still with one's own feelings. The magic of reclaiming your personal power, asking yourself what you desire and what you loathe. Inner peace is an exercise of steadily gaining control over the aspects of your life that seem to control you, such as anxiety, stress, mistreatment from others, and finances, to name a few. The boys have taught me to laugh more, share more, and not take things in life so seriously. To let go of the hard times and experience more joyful moments. What does that look like? Reframing a lifestyle, spending time with loved ones cultivating simple things with laughter at the dinner table, FaceTime calls, and conversations. Having confidence in yourself and your abilities to handle challenges with grace and to end up victorious, no matter what. To show compassion, patience, and grace to yourself when you are faced with something you might have once shied away from. Inner peace, to me, means accepting and knowing that I am only human, accepting my inner faults, and setting boundaries as a way to be in charge of my time. Other times, it means taking a break, be it sipping on a cup of coffee, taking a vacation, or going for a hike or walking in the park without any guilt. Perhaps now that my children are in their teens, these moments of respite and rest may seem further attainable. Truly though, the sooner we can reclaim inner peace the more readily we experience happiness.

## Happiness

In the hustle and bustle of life, evoking the chattels of happiness can sometimes feel daunting. It isn't a quick fix by taking a trip to

*woven*

the mall for the perfect outfit or getting a raise at work or looking outside yourself to find happiness. It isn't really about setting the goalpost for the next solution, the next job, the next house, or the salary increase because while those definitely can be rewarding, the novelty wears off after a while and you're still left feeling unfulfilled at a soul level. To me, true happiness is learning how to be more aware each day. Celebrating joy and contentment can be different for each one of us. I have found contentment comes from living in the moment and the peace of letting go of some of the anxiety or stresses, being grateful for the people I choose to spend time with, being kind to myself, helping others without expectation of reciprocation, and practicing meditation and mindfulness. I have learned to stop blaming myself. Accepting my humanness and the fallacies that come with it, I know that I might make decisions that I am not happy about and challenge my mind with the decision to let it go without any blame, guilt, or self-loathing. No longer will I censor myself or my thoughts to appease others. Freeing the mind feels good and living your best life feels better.

## Self-Love

Discovering how to practice self-love isn't an easy process; in fact, I am still learning. Self-love starts with you. Nurture yourself and discover the moments that make you feel refreshed, supported, and seen, and embrace them. Carpe diem the heck out of them, if you will! You can be happy right now, if you choose to be. You can love yourself more than anyone can, if you give yourself permission. The dishes can be done later, the laundry can be put away later, and the phone call can be returned later. If we take the time to self-nurture and self-love, it's a blissful harmony for the mind to be quiet, and we can find joy in little moments of the day. Practicing omitting the phrase "I will be happy when . . . " is a virtuous place to start. When we take accountability in offering ourselves delightful moments, we take charge of our own happiness. Sitting down with a cup of tea, journaling, going to bed twenty minutes earlier to read a book, meditating, taking a hot bubble bath, or even exercising, whatever it may be for you to practice self-love, know it is fostering your soul.

## Self-Worth

Do you ever wonder if you're worthy enough? Worthy of it? Worthy of your desires and needs? I have. I can shamelessly admit that over the last year or so, I started leaning into my worth. And once I started doing so, I never ever want to stop, ever again. Self-worth is an inner sense of sensitivity for being good enough, belonging with others, and being worthy of love. It isn't about what your friends, husband, or children think, or what a colleague may say, or a mentor may direct, but knowing self-worth comes from within, so *set it free*. Having self-compassion and the ability to be kind to yourself and less critical is one of the first steps. When we remember to give ourselves the same care and kindness as we would give to a friend, we set the tone on how we would like to be treated by others around us as well. From the ages of twenty-nine to fifty, I was defined by a lack of self-worth I had for myself. The desire to have a "normal" family because "I was going to do it right, not like my parents" was only a dream and not a reality. Instead, I suffered in the sadness of misaligned relationships for years, not knowing my worthiness, and my children witnessed the effects of it all. And still, there are some unturned stones that sit in the darkness of my soul. We all have value, worthiness, potential, and strength within. Reach for it. Find and embrace it because the suffering can end the sadness if you long for personal happiness. Stand in the mirror every day and tell yourself, "You are good enough, you are worthy, you are a Rockstar!" Say to yourself, "You have one life to live, and by God, girl, 'You have got this!'" Working with our own thoughts is not the most favorable undertaking. Convincing myself of the embracement to my own humanity, knowing no person is perfect, and working on the joy for self-improvement becomes a part of the routine for personal happiness. Focus on the positives of the future, only reflect on the mistakes, and be tolerant of yourself as you would be of others.

The persuasive soft voice expressively telling me to share the spirit of happiness, inner peace, self-love, and worthiness for my children is my purpose. To change my codependency. The desire to educate and put an end to the codependency cycle so my children don't repeat and look back or partake in the unworthy and sad unhealthy feelings I have is my purpose. Knowing and believing they are loved unconditionally. That is my purpose. To love and share change to those I love so dearly: my three little humans.

*A letter to my children,*

*Raising little humans isn't always an easy undertaking, but my gosh, it is a fulfilling one. From the day each of you were born, it was truthfully love at first sight. Loving another person is one thing, loving a child that was nurtured inside you and arrived in the world is an extraordinary experience of love, tears, joy, and happiness. You were planned and are forever loved unconditionally. The gift of having each other is just that: a gift that you have for so much of your life, so sanctify it. Your sweet little faces and big round eyes, your silly stories and funny words, your desire to be the greatest you in this demanding journey we call life make me so proud to be your mom. Your accomplishments, talents, athleticism, and drive for success in all that you do amaze me more than words can express. I have carried each of you along my own journey for years, encountering peaks and valleys of emotions, sunrises and sunsets no matter where we live, laughter and tears through the togetherness of family and friends, and all these experiences have taken me to the place I am today. I am in a place of inner peace and am taking moments to share my vulnerabilities. Understanding that you must know, and it is to be said that you are loved—you are so worthy of love. Each of you deserves happiness and inner peace and taking care of yourself is imposing a life of love for yourself. Be kind to yourself, your inner beauty, your soul. The embedded teachings to care for and have empathy for others first could raise a challenge in the assembly of your needs taking precedence. The yearning to have relationships that are healthier than your parents is natural and warranted. Don't suffer in sadness; instead, give yourself permission to flourish in love for yourself, celebrate joy and contentment while letting go of the "I will be happy when. . . ." Take time for self-nurture and self-love and give yourself permission for your mind to be quiet as you find joy in the little moments of each day. Be grateful for your strong friendships and let go of any judgment. Live in a place where your soul is happy, your thoughts are humbled, and you are in love with you. Because I can tell you and feel that I love you to the moon and back every night, but you have to believe it and share the wings of life to get there.*

*Love Always, your mom. xo*

# Chapter 8

# Adi Shakti—The Supreme Goddess

Sonali Thaker

*Sonali Thaker*

Sonali Thaker is wifey to her hubby, Harsh, proud mom to her son, Aarav, and a bird mom to Ray and Rio! Born and raised in India, Sonali followed her dream to settle in a foreign country ten years ago and has made Canada her home since. She attributes her creative genes to her literary and theater-practicing parents. Since the age of three, Sonali has performed more than 200 stage and television shows, presenting dance, drama, and emceeing events. She has won many accolades in creative writing, including *Mamas Who Write Coauthor Annual Scholarship* and has participated in public speaking and performing arts. While pursuing her degree, Sonali visited Japan as an exchange student. She captured her experiences in her first book, *Konnichiwa Japan — A Place Where Sun Rises & People Bow!*

Her blog, *Babies n Mii*, was inspired by the urge to help other first-time parents by sharing her pregnancy, maternity, and parenting journey. Her son called her "Mii," hence the name Babies n Mii! While on maternity leave, Sonali birthed a business venture that came to life. She picked the first initials from her husband, son, family, and her name, thus naming it *HATS Creations*!

Sonali is a full-time working mom and a conflict-resolution specialist. Sonali credits her immigration journey to Canada as a contributing factor in making her an empowering, strong woman. Her struggles with endometriosis are new waters, and she is learning to swim through with learnings from reading Bhagavad Gita. When she is not working, Sonali is watching TV or getting crafty with her son!

🌐 babiesnmii.ca

ⓕ @sonalithaker

◙ @babiesnmii

To my hubby, for unconditionally loving and supporting me for who I am. To my son, for being my courage and for whom I live each day more gracefully. To the two powerful women of my life: my late grandma **Baiya** and my mom for teaching me to chase my dreams. To my dad, for being my writing inspiration.

Lastly, to all endo-warriors for pulling along; trust me you are not alone.

"*Life cannot*, does not, and should not stop because of things that are beyond your control; however, you can carve a path that makes your life a little more enjoyable, consistent, and reliable."

# Adi Shakti—The Supreme Goddess

*When every hope is gone, when helpers fail and comfort flee, I find that help arrives somehow, from I know not where. Supplication, worship, prayer are no superstition; they are acts more real than the acts of eating, drinking, sitting or walking. It is no exaggeration to say that they alone are real, all else is unreal.*
–M.K. Gandhi, The Story of My Experiments with Truth

The magical moment I experienced four and a half years ago is still fresh in my mind. We experience life through moments, sensations, the feelings we feel through every second life continues to ebb and flow around us. Moments are life altering. The second I heard my son's first cry from behind the curtain in the operating room as my belly was surgically opened to allow this little human to enter the world and our lives was one such moment. I had carried my son for forty-one weeks and five days when I delivered him via cesarean section. A C-section was certainly not a part of my birth plan, but it was the only choice I had after my thirty-six-hour labor had made little-to-no progress. I was exhausted and swollen at every inch of my body. However, all the pain and uneasiness vanished when I first held my son, Aarav, in the recovery room and breastfed him. To me, in that instant, I became a mother. I know, some say women experience motherhood the moment they discover they're pregnant. For me, this transition from woman-hood to motherhood became real the moment I first held my son close and took in how he looked, how he felt, how he smelled, and how my body created and birthed this tiny human who is the embodiment of love.

Pregnancy changes a woman's body in many ways. I had heard this truth from many women around me, including my friends and family, but I only realized it when I became pregnant and birthed my little human into this world. I was in awe of how our bodies, as women, are powerful and strong and how they can create, nourish, and sustain life. I was the creator of his life, and this feeling left me feeling powerful. As a Hindu Brahmin woman, I felt the power of "Adi Shakti"—the Supreme Goddess within me. Yes, we are powerful indeed. And we can wield and weave this power and strength into all facets of our life.

As my motherhood journey began, I couldn't help but reflect on my pregnancy and my journey as a woman—an immigrant woman who would soon give birth to her baby, who would be a first generation Canadian. Life would be different for him or her. I knew it because I would ensure it was such. My thoughts drifted off to when I first set foot on Canadian soil and breathed its crisp northern air with a healthy dose of city air (but nothing like the smog-filled air in India, of course!).

Ten years ago, while in my early twenties, I bravely boarded the flight from Ahmedabad, Gujarat, India, to Toronto with high hopes and aspirations to study, work, and settle in this beautiful country—Canada. The only dream I nourished growing up was to move to a foreign country. It was a dream I cherished in the tiniest corner of my heart. Leaving behind family and friends wasn't easy, but I knew I was on this adventure to discover a place I could call my new home. It was easier said than lived. Life as an international student felt like a constant struggle to survive and to sustain. I waited tables, worked at a manufacturing plant, and worked at school.

Graduation was exciting, and with it came anxiety and challenges as I entered the corporate workforce. I had only two goals then: first to land a job and second to work toward my permanent residency (PR) in Canada so I could live there permanently. After multiple unsuccessful interviews, I landed a job, only to be laid off a few months later. At this point, all I cared about was landing a job that could help me pay my bills and student loan, and most importantly, so that I could apply for my PR in Canada. Luckily,

I landed another job.

As I navigated my way through my days of strife and struggle, I got engaged. Harsh and I were classmates in middle school and barely knew each other when we were younger. I changed schools, we lost touch with each other, and years later, we reconnected through some mutual friends. Let's say destiny brought us together, and the rest has been a fairy tale ever since. Summer 2014, we tied the knot, and he moved to Canada from the United States. That same year, I applied for my PR and waited patiently—all my hopes and dreams hanging in the balance of the final decision.

It had been a year and a half since I submitted my PR application. In 2016 I became pregnant with my son. With this news, our life was almost complete (the only outstanding part was my PR application approval, or at least we thought that way). The baby was timely and planned, as we were hoping to get our residency by the time I was due. I learned the hard way that the plans we have for ourselves often don't work the way we envision them to. Woody Allen once said, "If you want to make God laugh, tell him your plans." I was nine weeks pregnant when I received an email from Immigration, Refugees, and Citizenship Canada that changed everything. My PR application had been rejected; I would have to leave Canada in three months. All the hopes, dreams, and aspirations I came with were crushed within seconds. I thought to myself, *I am not ready to leave. I did not come here to go back.*

*woven*

*There was no second thought to this. I cannot leave; I do not want to leave. My life is here. This country is home to me, to us, to our soon-to-be-born baby.*

I was raised by my parents against the odds of society. They went against the status quo that was the Indian society and raised me to be ready to conquer the world, no matter what life threw at me. They had allowed me to pursue my interests without asking any questions. They supported my decision to come to a foreign country. *How could I just leave everything I had created here and head back?* I just couldn't stomach the thought of going back.

With my first child in my womb and crushed dreams in my heart, I decided to challenge the decision. I decided to fight back. A fight for my dreams, a fight for all the things I had let go in making this dream come true, a fight for countless things I appreciated about being in Canada, a fight to stay with my friends I had made, a fight to be recognized and respected for all the hard work I put into my job, and above all, a fight that would allow my child to be born in Canada. I didn't (and do not) want my son to experience the same struggle I did, fighting hard to live his dreams in another country.

I've never been a quitter. I've always found ways to adapt and thrive. I fail hard and fast and always seek the lesson within each experience. To me, failure holds the lessons and keys to our success. I viewed this challenge the same way.

I mustered a lot of courage from within and fought for myself and the life I envisioned I'd live in Canada. I knocked on every door I could. I sought legal help. I went to the court and appealed the decision. I applied for various immigration applications to stay in Canada. I failed, over and over again. But I did everything in my power to stay and bring my child into this world in Canada, the country I called "HOME." This was the country I identified with as *home*. The sleepless nights made me stronger every minute. When I talked to my unborn child, I told him to be strong and brave. I told him everything I was going through and that he had to be fearless. Away from our parents and family, my husband and I fought the battle all by ourselves. We both cried on each other's shoulders and wiped away our tears. But we had each other, which was half the battle won!

After 422 days of challenges, hurdles, numerous visits to the lawyer's office, multiple immigration applications, thousands of dollars spent from savings, uncounted tears, and delivering a handsome, healthy little human, good news struck our door. I won this battle. All that had fallen apart, fell in place. I finally got the status I was waiting for: Canadian PR. Three years later, I was overjoyed on the day I took the Citizenship Oath and became a proud citizen of Canada.

Armed with this experience in mind, I thought I would be totally prepared for everything that motherhood would bring my way— the good and the not-so-good moments. Afterall, if I could win the fight to stay in this country, I could win anything. At least I felt invincible. And the beautiful transition my body was going through as I continued my pregnancy made me feel like a powerful Goddess. I felt "Adi Shakti" circling within me and through me in each moment.

With an uneventfully healthy and normal pregnancy (minus severe morning sickness), I enjoyed my pregnancy and appreciated my body's ability to conceive and grow this life within me. The feeling was beyond belief. Every day, I was grateful to Mother Nature for blessing me with the power of being a woman and creating another human. Yet, nothing prepared me for just how much my body would change externally. I went from a size XXS to a size ten. Yes, I knew changes in the body were inevitable with pregnancy and childbirth, yet every time I thought about it, I felt uncomfortable. As excited as I was for my pregnancy and the beautiful journey of motherhood, I was equally overwhelmed with the rapid changes my body was going through. I had never gained more than 35 kilos of weight in my entire life (until twenty-four weeks into my pregnancy), which surprisingly doubled during my pregnancy. I loved my chubby cheeks and the belly bump. Everyone complimented me for my looks and how (good) different I looked. I blushed and loved all the attention.

I loved myself during those nine months. The itchy stretch marks around my waist and belly were my tiger stripes, my badges of honor, and my warrior marks that documented the growth of life within me and from me. I applied belly cream and vitamin E oil to soothe them and still continue this practice. I had always read that a lot of women experience postpartum depression; luckily, I did not feel that, but I had other struggles of my own. With my pregnancy being so normal and my son being in the perfect head-down position, my medical team and I hoped for a "normal" birth. I wasn't mentally prepared for a cesarean section until the night before I delivered my son, as my body tried to tell me that I may not deliver normally. I was ill prepared for it. Whatever little I knew about C-sections, I learned from my mom, as she delivered my sister and me surgically. To say my labor and delivery experience was traumatic would be stating it mildly.

Recovering from a cesarean section was challenging. I had to walk slowly, I couldn't walk up and down the stairs normally for about six months, and gone were the days where I could sit cross-legged on the floor. To top it all off, I started experiencing an undefined, concentrated pain on the left flank that would go through my pelvic floor and to my lower back. I did not need an epidural, but I had gotten a spinal block for the surgery, and so my complaints of the backache were complimented by pain medication.

As my son continued to grow, my pain attacks were a regular occurrence. When I had my first period after delivery, the pain

*woven*

level was a level twelve out of ten. I still remember crying on my bed, breastfeeding my son with my mom by my bedside. I told her I couldn't handle the pain. It was my first introduction with my heating pad, which is my best buddy today as not a day goes by where I don't use it. As the months progressed, my pain seemed to increase. The pain always showed up in the same region with the same symptoms—sharp, stabbing pain that felt like a never-ending ache. Unlike a headache that would disappear after a while (which typically resulted from sleep deprivation or exhaustion), this pain preferred to make a home within me and surfaced every single day like clockwork. I always thought I had a high pain threshold, since I'd navigated juvenile arthritis as a young teen and had kidney stones in the past. I highly doubt pregnancy would change my pain threshold.

Multiple follow-up appointments led to my doctor putting me under the knife again, which is how I found the answer to my pain. I was (presumptively) diagnosed with endometriosis. I had heard of it once before, as my sister had a surgery to remove a cyst, and it was suspected to be caused by endometriosis. Anxious and curious about it, I went online and started researching. I found the information about symptoms but nothing further on the cause or treatment. Although the surgery I underwent didn't reveal endometriosis, the doctor did remove an ovarian cyst and scar tissue from my cesarean.

Three months post-surgery, life felt good until the pain came back with a vengeance and we were back where it all started. I was living through painful times twice a month—ovulation and menstrual cycles were no different. Pain, pain, and more pain. Twenty-four hours a day, every single day. I was also diagnosed with five lumbar dislocated discs and recurring urinary tract infections to add to my pain and discomfort. It was now my new normal. By then, my concerns about my looks were long forgotten. I spent my workdays pretty much heavily medicated on painkillers and leaning on my heating pad for relief and support. At home, I would collapse in bed with my infant at 8:30 p.m. I couldn't muster up the physical strength to do anything else around the house, especially if I was commuting to work that day. At times, I lost hope within myself. I did not know how I could raise my son, continue to work and support my family, and live with chronic pain that left me feeling debilitated more days than none. My husband supported me in every way he could. He helped change the baby, cook meals, and put the baby to sleep. I felt so supported and seen by him. To this day, we parent our little boy equally and are very involved with him. Still, I desired to do something more to help myself feel better. I started physiotherapy as recommended to help with my back and to learn some exercises for my pelvic floor. I incorporated some exercise and was slowly getting back into shape. Almost two years into this journey, I was placed on

*woven*

hormone therapy as treatment for endometriosis. It was a presumptive treatment that did more harm than anything else. And I gained additional weight as a result. One year into hormone therapy, I chose to stop this treatment altogether and listen to my body yet again. She was always giving me signs to return home to myself, to be kind to myself, and to give myself much needed grace. At the time of writing this chapter, I still await another diagnostic laparoscopy. You might be wondering how I navigate my pain every single day? Three words: My son, Aarav. He gives me the strength to keep going when the days feel hard. He sees me for who I am.

When he was younger, I would breastfeed him to help me forget about my pain. It was the most soothing and calming time for me to hold my son close to my heart. It was Mommy and Aarav time—a time to connect and strengthen our bond. As he grew a little older, I'd find him by my side, kissing my cheeks and whispering, "I love you, Mama" every single time I'd have a pain attack and would lie on the couch. His words give me courage. The spark in his eyes while he kisses me is a promise, his way of telling me, "Mama, it is going to be okay. I am right here with you." His smile gives me power and courage to get back on my feet and fight for my health, my body. I talk to my body and tell her, "Body, I love you and want to help us feel better. You better be nice, as I have a long day at work, but more importantly, I have activities to do with Aarav." This self-talk gets me through. I used to be someone who couldn't sleep through the night if I added an inch around my waist. Instead, I would practice yoga rigorously until I got in shape. Today, I struggle to sit on the floor with my legs crossed for more than five minutes, but I still do it. I try to sit on the floor and play with my son, as it helps me stay present in the moment with him and focus on the joy I feel when we spend time together each day.

Living with chronic pain is not fun. There are a lot of unknowns. There are days that could be the absolute best while others could turn out to be nightmares. Lots of things are unpredictable. However, having lived with pain for close to five years, I know my triggers. It helps me plan my days and activities throughout the month. I know when to plan a full-day trip and when to try to be home in case I need to rest or lie in bed (almost all day).

I take these pain attacks as opportunities to better know myself. I engage in light exercises, yoga, and dancing when I feel better. Other times, I do arts and crafts with my son. And sometimes, I just stay in bed while watching my favorite show. Life cannot, does not, and should not stop because of things that are beyond your control; however, you can carve a path that makes your life a little more enjoyable, consistent, and reliable. Carving this path doesn't mean that pain doesn't exist. Pain exists, but you need to acknowledge it and find ways to work with it and ask for help and

*woven*

support to help you do so. I know it's easier said than done, but there is no shame in desiring to feel supported. No matter what it is you're going through. Talk to friends and family, ask for help, take medication if necessary, seek natural remedies, and hug your heating pad if that's what you need all day! Most importantly, educate people around you—about your illness, about your pain, what it can feel like, how it can present itself. Never underestimate the power of spreading awareness, as it can help them understand you a bit better, making things easier for all.

You are not your pain or your diagnosis, but you are your mindset. You are your approach to life and the challenges that it throws your way. Your body is a beautiful, strong, and nourishing force with which to be reckoned. Be gentle with it. Be gentle with yourself while still building your strength and perseverance. Focus on each life-altering moment and the good that it has to offer. And on days when it is incredibly hard to focus on all that is good, positive, and amazing about your life, remember this one thing: Your pain is your secret weapon—it is here to help you deepen your self-love, self-trust, and acceptance, while giving you the power to change your life, one small step at a time. As women, we have the power of the Divine and Powerful Goddess within us. Our stories are intertwined with each other, across borders, across cultures, across all generations. During the most difficult times of my life, one thing I never stopped doing was following my heart. I trusted myself more than anyone else. I believed in myself and my judgment. I wanted to prove that no matter where I come from, no matter how I look, and no matter if things, people, or situations put me into the ditch, I had the power within me to make things better for my family and me. My motto in life is "Life always throws you in the whirlpool, but instead of drowning by struggling to get out, stay calm, swim slowly, and get through. Life is certainly tough, but it is not unbeatable or unbearable. If you challenge it, you will also learn to win over it."

*woven*

# Chapter 9

# The Feisty Dance

Leanne Ford

*Leanne Ford*

Leanne Ford is first and foremost a mom of a very independent toddler who currently wants to do everything for himself. She is a registered social worker, perinatal mental health specialist, and a student affairs professional. Leanne is passionate about delivering an exceptional student experience and support for students throughout their academic journey, as well as supporting and treating mothers/parents through fertility, reproductive issues, pregnancy, postpartum, and the early days of becoming a parent.

Leanne strives to build awareness and capacity for mental health and wellness while also supporting complex student cases in her role at Canada's only women's university, Brescia University College, an affiliate of Western University. Additionally, she owns a part-time private counseling practice, which is part of a multidisciplinary team at Rebirth Wellness Centre Inc., a pre-and postnatal wellness clinic in London, Ontario.

When Leanne is not taking care of her toddler, spending time with her very supportive partner, friends or family, or working, you can find her collecting monarch eggs to raise butterflies, taking care of her forty-two plants, gardening, hiking, raising tadpoles, and/or enjoying a vanilla earl grey tea on her patio. She is truly passionate about her community, clean drinking water, humyn connectivity, learning, innovating, and nature.

 **@leanneford.mswrsw**

To my son, thank you for making me a mom. You are the experience I needed and wanted. I would give up my world a million times over to be in yours. When you arrived on this earth and it was finally time to meet you, I felt a love like never before. My son, you have my entire heart.

"*No matter* what path you took to become a parent, honoring that arrival is critical. Trust your becoming. Trust your intuition. Your truth. Your experience. This was the journey I had and the experiences I needed."

# The Feisty Dance

*The moment a child is born, the mother is also born. She never existed before. The woman existed, but the mother, never. A mother is something absolutely new.*

–Bhagwan Shree Rajneesh

Did you know that a big complication of childbirth is postpartum depression and anxiety? Did you know that one in seven women will experience postpartum depression or anxiety?[1] Did you know that one to two cases out of 1,000 births will experience a more serious perinatal mood and anxiety disorder, like psychosis?[2]

I was one of those statistics.

I never thought I would be sitting in the emergency room with my own mother nine days postpartum asking her if there were babies crying or if I was hearing things. As I looked around the emergency room, I saw someone familiar to me. It was a former coworker; this was my worst nightmare. I didn't want them to ask why I was there. I remember walking by them without making eye contact when I heard, "Leanne? Is that you?" No make up, no bra, breast milk leaking through my shirt, hair a mess. As I quietly said hi, they asked, "What are you here for?" I tried to change the subject and then ended up lying. I said, "I am here to get my incision looked at. I had a cesarean." This "lie" was somewhat true. Just four days prior, I had been to the emergency department for my incision from the belly birth because it was infected and leaking a straw-colored, disgusting-smelling fluid. As I sat there and waited for my name to be called for a mental health assessment, I hoped and wished that I wouldn't see anyone else I knew. Shame and embarrassment bubbled up. I felt as naked as a baby, so exposed and vulnerable. *I should know what to do and how to cope with all the negative thoughts I am experiencing. I should be able to get back into my window of tolerance and be able to manage this life change because I help people do it every day. That is my job! I am a registered social worker. I'm a helper.*

Before I get into the depth of my experience with postpartum depression, anxiety, and psychosis, I want to share with you who I was before I became a mother. This information is important to understand because I thought I needed to keep these identities separate and quiet. I didn't know how much becoming a mother would change my being. Mental health stigma kept me from sharing my humanness. Before I was a mother, I was a partner, daughter, sister, friend, and social worker. I loved being outside in nature, doing crafts, creating, exploring, being curious, connecting with friends, and gardening. I was a career woman. I focused on my relationships, but I also loved to work and put energy into things that brought me joy! Some say it may have been a trauma response because I never wanted to sit with my own thoughts and always kept busy, but it's just how I was. I always had a project on the go. I felt called to show up and provide service to others. Boy, was I naïve. I had no idea what motherhood had in store for me: the selflessness it would demand, the sleep deprivation, the deep love and gratitude for the opportunity to be a mother. And the ambivalence. It cracked me open, and I was left with no choice but to continue to do shadow work that was, quite literally, being pulled out of me.

Becoming a mom was an idea and role I always knew I wanted, but what I didn't know was the ambivalence that would come along with becoming a mom. Matrescence is the transition into motherhood. Similar to the transitionary period into adolescence, some experience an identity crisis when they enter motherhood. Matrescence is about the physical, physiological, and emotional changes that we experience as a result of birthing our children. Becoming a mom changed my whole being and brought me great love and joy; however, I was under prepared for the feisty dance between bitter resentment and deep gratification that I would experience. This dance is ambivalence. It's loving your child more than you have loved anyone else in the whole world, but also not loving motherhood all the time. It's wanting to pull out your hair when your baby is crying, or wishing you were anywhere else during the sleepless nights and colicky days, *and* also feeling like if anything ever happened to your baby, you couldn't continue living. It's sending your child to daycare when you are home on vacation because you need a break but missing them when they are gone. It's wanting time to speed up and slow down at the same time. It's counting down the hours and minutes until bedtime and then the second you leave their room, you miss them and scroll through your phone, looking at photos of your sweet child(ren). It's loving my tiny human more than I could have ever imagined and also missing my life and what it felt like before I had this type of selfless responsibility. This gray zone of motherhood was deeply confusing, and I felt under prepared for the ambivalence that was so prominent. Intensive mothering norms have created a culture where parents do not talk openly about the ambivalence they experience for fear of being judged, fear of being seen as a failure, fear of not being a "good enough" mother. It is especially true for those who have experienced different paths to becoming a parent, such as navigating fertility challenges, surrogacy, parents who choose to adopt, LGBTQ+ same-sex parents who can't conceive on their own, and/or people who need to do IUI or IVF. It altered the way I needed to show up in the world and forced me to be present daily while challenging my patience and personal values. It's a type of love like no other. I always knew change was upon us as we entered parenthood, but I held on hard to what was before I became a mother. Nothing anyone tells you and no prenatal class can ever prepare you for what to expect when becoming a mom.

On August 27, 2018, I gave birth to a beautiful baby boy. My pregnancy and creating life within me were unbelievable. I was supported by my mom at the beginning of my labor and my husband during the remainder of the labor and birth. We had an unplanned cesarean after twenty-four hours of labor and "failure to progress." Being in the hospital for three days after delivering the baby allowed us the appropriate time to manage pain and any complications from major surgery. It wasn't until we were going to be discharged on day three that I was flooded by anxiety and all the intrusive, negative thoughts began: *What did we get ourselves into? I don't know how to take care of a baby. What if I can't get him to stop crying? I don't feel connected to him. My milk isn't in, so how will I know he is getting enough?*

Returning home with a baby was wild. We had a tiny human who was depending on us to take care of him. My mood and thoughts only got worse. I didn't feel an immediate connection with my baby, and I was in physical pain. All I wanted to do was sleep, but I couldn't settle. My mind was too busy worrying. I couldn't stop crying. The postpartum anxiety and depression that I experienced presented by being controlling, telling my husband what to do and how to do it, not letting family or friends hold the baby, avoiding going out for fear of the baby crying in public, worrying about my incision and thinking I was dying, fixating on the swelling in my legs and feet postpartum (which was caused by having an epidural), calling the midwifery clinic's after-hours line multiple times for reassurance, crying uncontrollably, being irritable picking fights, and having the sensation that my body was buzzing and heart was racing, which was made worse by no sleep and night sweats.

When the adrenaline wore off and things settled, my body started to steep in the tea of motherhood. The swelling went down, my incision started to heal, and my body was no longer sore from the epidural shakes. Some of you might be wondering what happened in those first nine days postpartum to land me in the hospital, separated from my newborn baby. I've described my symptoms, but how did these take root? I felt really disconnected from reality and from my baby. I felt like an imposter when I initiated breast-feeding, as though I had no clue what I was doing. Public health nurses came to visit twice to try and help with latching, which was helpful for education purposes, but I just couldn't get my baby to latch and was told my milk supply was low.

*woven*

Midwives were at our house often, attempting to help me with breastfeeding, weighing the baby, and checking my incision. As I sat on the couch and cried, tears streaming down my face, my midwife asked me how I was doing with the transition to having a baby. I asked my midwife if she wanted me to be honest. I said, "I hate this. I want my old life back." Saying those words out loud to my midwife took vulnerability. I was worried what she would think of me as a mother and a person. In hindsight, I didn't hate my baby, I hated that I was "failing" and wasn't able to figure it out. My perfectionism was being tested. I then proceeded to tell the midwife that I was constantly hearing the baby crying when he wasn't, which was causing me not to sleep. She listened so gently and asked if I was experiencing any hallucinations or delusions. I gave her a funny look because I didn't want to tell her. I tried really hard to keep this part to myself because I know what comes next and didn't want to admit I needed help. I was worried that if I asked for help and was honest about how I was feeling, I would be seen as incapable. As I looked down, I told her that I had woken up in the middle of the night. I was rocking my baby, and I'd thought my husband put the baby on me to sleep/breastfeed. When I got up the next morning, I got upset with my husband and asked him to check with me before he placed the baby on me to sleep, but he said that it had never happened. I told her that I was hearing auditory hallucinations of all sorts of baby noises, but I'd never heard anything that told me to hurt the baby.

According to the health professionals, my condition was considered a medical emergency. I, of course, resisted and told my midwife that I just needed to sleep. My husband was incredibly supportive throughout this journey, in spite of having started a new job just days after I gave birth. I was surrounded by family and friends who wanted to help and offered to watch my baby while I napped. Despite the offers, my nervous system was so wound up, and the intrusive and unwanted thoughts kept coming. I had a deep desire to control everything, from people holding my baby to changing how my anxiety manifested. I had intrusive thoughts like *What if he stops breathing? What if my mom drops him or faints while she is caring for him? My husband doesn't know his cries and won't know what he needs. My baby needs me and only me. I can't stand his crying, so I shouldn't take a break. What if I just went for a drive and never came back? I could leave right now and the baby would be fine with my husband; no one would miss me.*

Our midwife made a plan with my husband and me and strongly urged me to attend the hospital to get a mental health assessment. With eyes red and burning from crying, I didn't want to believe this situation was happening to me. After consulting with my therapist who I hadn't seen in a few years, I decided to go to the hospital and get the mental health assessment because although I knew the signs of perinatal mood and anxiety challenges, my brain was foggy, and I was in the mud. I was not at my best and was mentally unwell. I needed help beyond what I could give myself. As I sat across from the triage nurse at the hospital with tears streaming down my face, she asked me where my baby was as if I had done something wrong. I told her that he was safely at home with his dad. I could tell that the nurse was compelled to say something to assuage the pain, but she refrained. I was triaged quite quickly, as true postpartum psychosis needs to be treated as soon as possible. Since my education training lies in mental health and wellness, I knew that lack of sleep could be a contributing factor for experiencing delusions and/or hallucinations. When I met with the mental health nurse and the on-call doctor, I requested that I be prescribed the lowest dose of Lorazepam to use as needed and that we create a plan for my husband and mom to care for my baby while I rested and got sleep over the next few days. I truly felt that if I were able to sleep and manage my anxiety with medication, then I could stabilize and start to feel better. Since I didn't have thoughts of hurting myself or my baby, I didn't believe anyone was trying to hurt my baby and me, and I was well aware of the date, time and place, the doctor agreed to initiate a solid plan for me and prescribed a low dosage for me to take as needed.

The doctor's response was the golden ticket. Typically, if someone is experiencing psychosis, they are "formed" and have to involuntarily stay in the hospital for two weeks. If this psychosis happens during the postpartum period, they are separated from their baby. Sleep can make a significant impact on mental health and functioning. Prior to visiting the hospital, I hadn't slept more than two consecutive hours in days. Part of the discharge plan was that I needed to follow up with an outpatient psychiatrist within a week while I waited for an initial appointment with the perinatal psychiatrist my midwife referred me to prior to my going to the hospital. I also had support from my midwives, and they continued to visit once a week to check on my son and me. I started to engage in regular therapy again as well as had public health nurses and family home visitors from the local health unit come weekly to support me with anything I needed. My husband had just started a new job and couldn't take much time off, so I depended on my mom to drive me to appointments (because I couldn't drive for about a month and a half after my cesarean), to come over a couple hours a day to watch the baby so I could shower, have a break, and to help with anything else I needed. My mom would often encourage me to go nap after having a sleepless night, and I would try to, but my mind was busy and my body was buzzing, so I would end up doing a guided meditation to rest my mind and attempt to calm my body. To say I had a village surrounding me is an understatement. My support and protective factors allowed me to recover well and continue the critical maintenance of my own mental health and well-being daily.

*woven*

Being a social worker and psychotherapist in the helping profession, I believe there is an added layer of mental health stigma because you are "supposed" to know how to cope with big life changes and mental health struggles. It is our training and what we do for a living. No matter how much I grow and gain experience as a social worker, it never seems to get easier to ask for help. It is easy to think that social workers and/or therapists "have it all together." The reality is that we are human, and struggle is part of the human experience. As I reflect on why this added layer of stigma exists, I have come to realize that there is a harmful discourse of "us versus them" that pervades our life. Typically, you don't hear or see helping professionals telling their own personal stories of their childhood experiences or their struggles as they became who they are today in their professional identity because there is a sense that you shouldn't really talk about these sorts of things or "self-disclose," thus reinforcing the "us versus them" notion: *Helpers and healers are the "healthy ones" who are all-knowing, and clients are the ones who need to be fixed and healed because they are the "ill" ones.* Not true, at all.

If your mental health is languishing, then there is a perception that you are not qualified to be a mental health practitioner or a helper. There is a real fear that as someone in the helping profession that ability or "fitness" to practice could be questioned, which could affect our registration and licensing to practice with regulatory bodies. The personal becomes political. It is the dominant discourse that contributes to my shame, and it needs to change. Untangling ourselves from the stories that keep us trapped and deconstructing those we've outgrown is important. I am very good at what I do, *and* I have the integrity and insight to know when my mental health is languishing and identify when breaks and extra support are required so that I can maintain my own mental health. Having life experiences of struggle have made me a better social worker and therapist. They have created an opportunity for me to better relate to the people I serve and to walk alongside them in their journeys of healing. Who I am flows into all identities and use of self in clinical work. I've come to learn and appreciate that these identities cannot be separate. The reality is that we are all going to struggle because it's part of the human experience. The real work comes from how you manage the struggle and whether you choose to build resilience as a result of that struggle.

I also want to acknowledge my privilege and knowledge as a mental health professional myself. I am extremely privileged to have been surrounded by an amazing village as well as to have the skills/knowledge to help me through what I experienced as a difficult time. Mental health does not discriminate. Everyone has mental health and can experience languishing mental health challenges in the perinatal period, despite your professional identity, socioeconomic status, race, culture, and/or if you have had previous pregnancies and/or births. But here is what I would love for you to anchor into:

- You are not your thoughts or feelings, and they do not define you or your journey.
- Reaching out for help early on and at any point is brave and important.
- We are human, and although struggle is a part of the human experience, we don't have to suffer in silence.
- It's not about *if* you will struggle and need help, it is about *when*.
- If you are a helper, start by helping yourself first. Self-care needs to be a priority and is critical in helping others.
- Check in on your strong friends. Yes, just like that meme we see on social media. Check on them. Just because they are high functioning doesn't mean they couldn't use some respite, a hot meal, tea delivery, and/or an offer to come over and help clean house / do laundry.
- When someone shares a healing story like mine, they aren't looking for you to feel sorry for them. If you aren't sure what to say, here are some ideas: "I can see you have come a long way in your healing and growth," "It is evident that you are brave for sharing this part of your story and being vulnerable is courageous," "Thanks for sharing your truth;

it resonates," "You are breaking down barriers and challenging dominant discourses!"

- When a baby is born, a mother is also born. We need to mother ourselves with love, kindness, and care.
- Being proactive and having a contingency plan for when things go awry can be important in minimizing distress. If you have preexisting mental health concerns or other risk factors, consider meeting with a registered therapist, doula, midwife, and/or other primary health provider to create a postpartum plan. Proactive coping is gold.

Strong mama, all that energy you're putting toward trying to be okay could be going toward restoring your vibrancy, investing your strength selectively, and making the kind of difference you're here to make. Where I am now feels nothing short of amazing. I am so honored every day that my son chose me to be his mama. Every day, I continue to practice patience and self-compassion, and I continue to learn from him. One of my biggest lessons on this journey thus far is to be the mother my son needs instead of being fixated on getting it right all the time. Allowing myself to let go of unrealistic expectations of what society expects a mother to be or do is really freeing. Reclaiming our power starts with learning to shift our perception about the stories we adopt, internalize, perpetuate, and build our lives, world view, and sense

*woven*

of self around, then release them. My mental health has been managed and continues to be maintained by accessing therapy for myself when needed, leaning on my supports, utilizing my care team of multidisciplinary practitioners, asking for help, taking supplements to help manage mood, utilizing clinical supervision to process counter transference, and practicing my proactive coping strategies and preventative measures for flourishing mental health and well-being. I tried to hide behind the truth of who I was for so long and felt that I needed to keep my personal and professional life separate because of the stigma that people in the helping profession encounter. The moment my baby was born, I was a changed woman, and my identities of mother and social worker transformed in a beautiful way. I was able to relate to people with new depth, and we all know relatability in the therapeutic relationship is fundamental. I knew my purpose was in helping those around me, and I needed to start doing that by helping myself first. It only took having a baby to make that happen! My hope is that by sharing my experience, it allows other women, particularly other helping / health care professionals and caregivers, to know they aren't alone, to squash stigma, to build their village, and to seek help early on to prevent and/or manage mental health challenges for better long-term outcomes. There is community in connection and shared experiences, so share your story or a piece of it! I guarantee there is at least one other person who will resonate. Being able to connect with someone on this level is healing in itself.

While my experience is my own unique narrative of my truth, becoming a mom and/or caregiver isn't always met with significant mental health challenges. There is joy in motherhood and how it intersects with other parts of my life. You are a good-enough woman. You are a good-enough mother. And no, you are not being over dramatic. Your mental health matters and is not something to be trivialized or stigmatized. You deserve to feel well. No matter what path you took to become a parent, honoring that arrival is critical. Trust your becoming. Trust your intuition. Your truth. Your experience. This was the journey I had and the experiences I needed. It is not a reflection of who I am as a mother and/or social worker. We don't learn when things are easy. We learn from struggle and build resilience from there. Being a parent or caregiver is one of the most selfless roles anyone could ever take on. The power is within me and in each and every one of you.

With deep gratitude,

Leanne

# *Chapter 10*

## Mi Amor

LISA TOWN

*Lisa Town*

Lisa Town is a forty-year-old womxn with a story about searching for the holy grail of life like the majority of us. She resides in beautiful Whitby, Ontario, roughly forty-five minutes east of Toronto, and she has done so for most of her life (minus a brief hiatus to attend the University of Waterloo). She has a son, a career, a dog, a house, friends/family, a well-used student classification subscription to Spotify, and an abundance of craft beers in her fridge. Lisa considers herself very blessed and eternally grateful, and she is always on a quest to find the next best version of herself, while helping humanity along the way.

@painthelisatown

For Mom and Dad who influenced my everything. xo

"After that day, I was intrigued and began attentive yet cautious assessments, hoping to understand who and what you were all about."

# Mi Amor

*I have a confidence about my life that comes from standing tall on my own two feet.*
-Jane Fonda

You walked by the construction site on that hot July day, perfectly disheveled the first time I noticed you. There were rumblings about your new singleness in the neighborhood, but we had not had the opportunity to formally meet. Some said you were recently separated, others questioned if your husband had passed away. Regardless, your availability caused quite a stir and came as a surprise to many. You were wearing a white dress with little black flowers all over it, bright red lipstick, and blue converse Chucks. It's shorter now, but at the time, your shoulder-length hair was messy and looked uncombed or it just could have been the humidity that day. The dress was a little bit sheer from the sun and really

183

showed off the contours of your curvy body that had given birth to a young son just a few years before. There was a lackadaisical confidence about your saunter. You weren't carrying anything like a purse or grocery bags, and it wasn't obvious where you were going, but you held a small smile, and you looked happy. There was something uplifting about you. There must have been ten or more workers on site ferociously attempting to fix whatever town ailment needed to be attended to when you walked by. As you passed, not one head looked up from the work. There was not a single inappropriate comment, lingering stare, or insolence as expected. All the workers carried on with their tasks as though nothing was occurring and everything was as it should be. However, as you walked farther down the road with your back safely toward the group, you kicked a small rock, and every worker's head followed you all the way down the street as you walked away. The Queen had arrived, and the people had come to receive her with lowly eyes and admiration.

After that day, I was intrigued and began attentive yet cautious assessments, hoping to understand who and what you were all about. When you were alone, your activities were relatively predictable. You woke in the early mornings, turned on minimal lights only as needed, and prepared multiple cups of tea, bag in. Weekdays were spent devotedly attached to computer screens in your art-covered home office, typing and talking away, utilizing a

*woven*

variety of tones and facial expressions depending on the day. It was noticeable that your professional capacity was a very important piece of your existence because there were many hours dedicated to that office space. Evenings and weekends were slightly interchangeable. Sometimes you would leave for hours with a paddle board or yoga mat in tow, returning with groceries, Value Village bags, or just a general expression of fatigue from some outdoor adventure you had partaken in. Other times you could be spotted with a writing utensil, paint brush, or book in hand, either in front of the warm glow of a fireplace in the winter or sitting quietly on your porch in warmer months, always with your dog underfoot and a pint glass nearby. The television was rarely on, and outdoor exercise was a routine. Bedtime was, for the most part, fairly early, which likely coincided with the early rise. Spiritual rituals such as smudging and prayer occurred on the regular, and there was peacefulness about your persona after those moments of gratitude occurred.

Despite your patterns, you had some eccentric habits and a very interesting yet confusing combination of a type A and type B personality. On garbage collection days, recycling bins were overflowing with toilet paper rolls, clothing labels, and whatever scraps could possibly be reutilized. Beer and wine empties were always placed on the top for first-come, first-served collectors, and sometimes you would run them out to folks on bikes to gift them accordingly. The compost bin was filled with dryer lint, hair, string, food scraps, and leftover cooking oils, and it was turned on the regular. Anything that had the possibility of regrowth, such as green onions, celery, or lettuces found their lanky bodies plunked in water and replanted, weather permitting. Random items marked as free and usually with some other quirky note like "I'm a little bit rusty, but I still work" emerged from the storage space and were placed most suitably on the side of the road for any passerby to pick up. As soon as the snow melted and the sidewalks were thawed, an old English bulldog without a leash would arise like a ground-hog and cruise the block sans leash with you sans shoes, a pairing quite content to turtle around the block without the restrictions of armor and the earth underfoot. The same philosophy applied to clothing. Many times, you sat protected by your backyard, sunning yourself casually, reading, listening to music, drinking beer, and swimming without a bathing suit. In the evenings, and lights out in the home, it was almost guaranteed that you would raid your freezer for Kawartha Dairy without any type of covering. Pajamas were reserved for late afternoons or early evenings and were not necessarily appropriate sleepwear, in accordance with you. The beginnings of spring signified open windows and the sounds of the Rolling Stones heard blaringly around the block. What seemed like hundreds of Persian rugs, colorful pillows, and houseplants would be lovingly strewn on the porch, and you could be seen in

*woven*

a full-blown cleaning frenzy, dancing around and singing along with totally incorrect self-declared lyrics.

My favorite observation of you was when the paint brushes or writing utensils came out and the complicated artistic relationship appeared in all its chaotic splendor. Like a mad conductor leading the orchestra, you wildly applied the same premise to your personal experiences with art. On good days, canvas, wood, scraps of paper, paints, pencils, and photos became intertwined as one beautiful hypothesis. Other times, there was a more opposing somber tone to your creative experiments, and the imaginative endeavors were not as easy to tap into. Those canvases and pages stood alone, untouched and derelict for months sometimes, but they usually submerged later after a more introspective period of your life, and, in many instances, they became your most beautiful works. As you created, there was usually the presence of auditory accompaniment, and you have a very eclectic musical taste that spans across all genres and generations depending on the day. Podcasts, audiobooks, or fielding customer service-related calls were not as promising and usually signified frustration, grasp at stimulus or inspiration, or simply your heart was not in the work on that particular day for whatever reason, probably because the piece was not connecting with the psyche or the soul, which was what art was all about to you.

You were not always alone though, and your art usually reflected a particular muse. There were a handful of suitors by the house, certainly not in droves, and there were a few consistent groups of other guests who joined you from time to time. However, there was a very significant presence of a small, energetic, dark-haired boy who was looked upon with so much love, admiration, and devotion and without a shadow of a doubt was your most prized and precious accomplishment and heir to the throne. Together, your son, dog, and you displayed the most wonderful relationship, sitting on the porch cuddling up, reading, watching the laptop, and eating cereal in the morning like a little pack. In the afternoons, the sidewalk chalk, Nerf guns, and swimming-pool-splashing-induced laughter could be heard around the neighborhood. At night, the sparklers came out to compete with the fireflies and stars that filled the sky, and on occasion, the wolf pack could be heard howling at the moon. There was a high expectation around manners, and all passersby received a warm, harmonized hello, smile and wave, or a thumbs-up. Generally, your legs were covered in dirt, bruises, and scrapes from the explorations of the day into forests, streams, and beaches. Many times, the unleashed, naked foot totters around the block expanded to include all three of you, and your adventurous, carefree, gypsy spirits captivated those around you with some neighbors poking their heads through covered windows to catch a glimpse of your happy expressions that radiated beyond your presence.

*woven*

Observations and assessments continued for some time longer and then it was determined that it was time to begin our more formal introductions. A few months after the beginning of the pandemic seemed to be an appropriate time to make your acquaintance, and we finally worked up the courage to do so. It was interesting how our connection began with a private piece of you that was not as carefree as what had been presented so many times before. On this particular day, you were sobbing uncontrollably, talking to God, head and heart respectfully on a colorful prayer mat placed on the floor. You were describing your experiences with grieving, loss, and loneliness. You missed your mother, father, and the family unit and networks from before the separation. You used to be so confident about your existence and your path, and now you could feel the ground shaking, quivering beneath you—your very sense of being questioned, marred with doubts about who you were and what you were supposed to be doing going forward. Guilt accompanied conversations that you were the one solely responsible for the deterioration of your marriage. Despite the pain in your voice, gratitude was clearly pronounced, and it was evident you respected God's plans for you, and you would move toward them willingly, despite your fears and apprehensions. There was a beautiful vulnerability around this moment, and I knew right then and there that I was hopelessly falling in love with you.

Our soulful introduction led to an amazing friendship, built upon trust, respect, and womanly intuition. Storytelling occurred on the regular, and your accounts were mapped out on paper before they had a chance to be shared. Although you had participated in many emotional and spiritual healing practices over the years, you safely continued to unpack and cleanse some of the situations from your past that were no longer serving you. Your childhood and youth were very blessed, and your parents were conservative hippies who were cultured, patriotic, and philanthropic. They did everything to both provide for and diversify you in so many ways, but there was also a sadness that peppered the experience and forced you to grow up in a forceful way before you were ready to progress to the next maturation stages. Your father was a multi-layered individual who was beyond brilliant, incredibly cool, and well liked, but a dark cloud was always on his tail, imposing a contradictory personality who also lived with a moderately regulated, self-maintained mental health infliction. This instability was very confusing for you as a young person, and you spent many years trying to make sense of a dichotomized childhood. Your mother immigrated to Canada from Mexico at a young age and lived with her adoptive German father (Opa) and biological Mexican mother (Oma) and two brothers. Their immigration experiences were well marbled with hardships, and life was extremely challenging for the family as your mother grew up and entered the 1970's womanhood and married life. Somehow,

*woven*

your mother managed to whittle her way through the dense forests placed in front of her and created a magical compartment of childhood for both your sister and you. Although there was lots of love present in your parents' marriage, similar trials would arise, and there was an element of symbiotic, secretive dysfunction in your childhood home. You were inadvertently desensitized to your circumstances and encouraged not to share your experiences, as they were personal to the family. You had an experience of living with privilege from the periphery, on one hand lacking nothing, and on the other, feeling fractured. As you aged, you viewed this unique experience to be a blessing in disguise because it allowed a sense of understanding and sympathy for humankind in general. The personal was the political in your world and therefore, allyship was a very important component of your existentialism.

Your mother received her cancer diagnosis, and a few weeks later she was gone. This period of time in your life was both chaotic and destabilizing. Not only were you trying to process unimaginable grief and maintain a marriage and professional aspirations, but you also felt an extreme responsibility around your father's well-being and transitioned from daughter to guardian, once again skipping the natural role progression with no preparedness. The years following your mother's death were riddled with angst. Your father was now left afloat to function, and that functioning was many times conducted in an unhealthy manner. The roller-coaster ride was relentless, so relentless that you were supposed to attend a hockey game with your husband one Valentine's Day, but instead you were enmeshed in a labor of love in the emergency room, convincing both the psychologist and your father to get a ticket for the best ride in town, the psychiatric unit where he finally gained admission for several weeks. Although you didn't realize it at the time, you had become a human pin cushion, and each experience had created a deep hole in your personal foundation that was very quickly becoming filled with cement. Similar to your childhood, you reverted to a disturbing and secretive pattern of managing alone and not sharing experiences with anyone, not even your husband at the time. You were hardening, and you didn't even know it.

Several years following these experiences and a beer-induced trip to France, Belgium, and Holland, you learned you were pregnant with that willful, most gorgeous, brown-haired boy. You and your husband were elated by the news and were so excited to share it with family and friends. The pregnancy was worrisome, as ultrasounds revealed your son had some fluid on the brain that could be correlated to future health concerns. Your husband and you rallied during this time with such positive and optimistic force, and you psychologically blasted that baby with nothing but good vibes. When he finally arrived in the world, twenty-four hours later by emergency cesarean section, every sedative you could

*woven*

humanly consume and a whole lot of Rolling Stones love, he was perfect and filled your life with so much energy and purpose. You then shared a secret you had told no one. Although you were elated with motherhood, there was an oppositional force that also presented itself in a sense of trepidation unlike anything you had experienced before. You felt an uncontrollable deficiency and incompetence around mothering. Your model, who was supposed to be your mother, was gone, and her generational wisdom was unreachable. That acknowledgment was heartbreaking for you. The realization of being a motherless mother sparked a period of postpartum anxiety in which control could only be garnered through unusual practices such as excessive cleaning, gardening, organizing, and skipping sleep. Really, it was anything that could take you away from the feeling of pain and fear and replace it with a task to focus on. Once again, your voice was muffled through the experience, and you chose to keep the information to yourself until you had no choice but to seek professional help. The cement that had filled the pin cushion was solidifying very quickly.

Several years went by, and you had learned to move past some of your worries around motherhood, as you had proven to yourself that you not only enjoyed the role but you were also mastering it. It was a lovely experience caring for your son and providing all the love you could to him. You were not able to juggle all the balls, though, as your father was still acting out and generally behaving erratically. One day, you had a visit from your adored in-laws and your husband, who was working at the time. Their expressions said it all, and you knew what was coming before you heard the words "he is gone." You didn't cry because you had forgotten how to do that. Instead, you responded, "Thank God," and you meant it genuinely and not sarcastically in the slightest. You weren't grateful that he had chosen to end his life, you were grateful because of the awareness of torment he had experienced and tried to find solutions for, and he was now at peace and with your mother whom he missed so dearly. You made a very conscientious choice at that point to officially harden. You would not nor were you able to share your emotions or process any of the heartache that had been pent up for years. Nothing was going to hurt you anymore because you were impenetrable from any more pain. Hard as a rock.

Work, parenting, and life continued after that. You continued to excel and achieve and moved through additional education and training. You had now lost your mother, your father, and a few other key people in between, while moving through life quite quickly. But nothing could prepare you for the loss that would leave you feeling gutted. "I don't love you anymore," said your husband with a very confident and unfamiliar expression on his face. You were frozen in disbelief and unable to make sense of the statement. Shortly after, he left permanently, and you,

*woven*

recently divorced, have remained at arm's length ever since. So many things. So many contributing factors. Even today, there are so many unanswered questions that you will probably never have the answers to. Perhaps he doesn't have them either. At this point, the center could not hold anymore, and you officially exploded and would need to be put back together in a completely new version of yourself that would require kindness, patience, perseverance, and courage because it was not going to be easy. This point is when I officially fell in love with you. The vulnerability and courageousness I had first witnessed on that colorful prayer mat was now ready to metamorphosize into something that was already perfect to begin with.

Of course, there were so many elements of you that were appealing once divulged. There were hours and hours spent untangling years of silence to the point where your voice was enunciated and unwavering. You found a way to mix all your skills and abilities into a perfect circle where all could be utilized. You were sexy, passionate, and full of zest, and you held an intense desire to travel and explore as soon as the world would permit. You worked hard in all elements of your life, and you had certainly spent the time to understand your values around creativity, curiosity, empathy, and solitude, and you had a deep love and respect for Mother Earth (which explains the unusual recycling and small urban farming routines). You were built upon a strong foundation of God, family, and friends who picked you up and carried you throughout your experiences, and nothing was achievable without them. Those who loved you prior to your losses and divorce loved you even harder after, and their power, prayer, and energy was relentless and kept you above water. Most attractive of all, you spent lots of devoted time with the brown-haired boy who continues to be the most important source of happiness for you, and your casual dispositions complement one another well.

I've thought many times over the last year or so about the first day I noticed you and have concluded that those workers did not look up from their work to even hint at objectification because you demanded it. It was obvious that there was an expectation of dignity and respect simply by the way you walked with a comfortable air of regal yet unassuming confidence that exemplified a womxn comfortable in her own skin. You didn't know where you were going that day, but you have come to understand that it will be uncovered as you listen and explore it. You will never forget where you came from. You are selective in both your friendships and partnerships, and it's obvious you are conducting tryouts sparingly and critically. Your next intimate relationship will be organic, communicative, and redemptive this time around, and there's no rush to settle for anything less because you already have a kingdom. You are an unusual concoction of a beast, and although life has not always been easy, you have accepted your

*woven*

happily dilapidated existence and found a way to repurpose your pain in all its glorious splendor into something truly beautiful and inspirational, and you are satiated with life. I look forward to meeting every version of you as I move along my path, mi amor (my love). Welcome home, to yourself. Welcome to the first day of the rest of your life.

Love,

Lisa (your evolved, still eccentric, and very passionate self)

xo

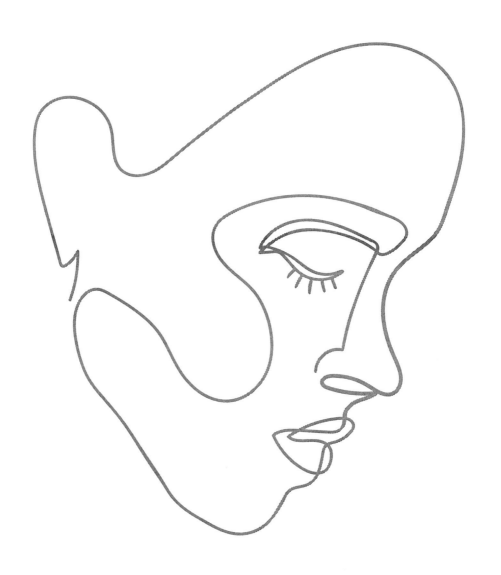

*Section 3*

# HOMECOMING

DR. PARASTOO BOROUMAND

AMY SYED

JENNIFER DE ROSSI

MICHELLE NICOLET

SHERRI MARIE GAUDET

EMILY EDWARDS

TANIA JANE MORAES-VAZ

Homecoming. Do you remember what it feels like? A celebration, a reverie, and a transformation happening simultaneously. Kinda like those pep rallies or spirit days we had in high school. Where the jocks were worshiped, the cheerleading squad cheered them on, the entire community celebrated them. No matter the wins or losses. And if they lost a game, the support that poured out from everyone around them felt like one big collective hug. That is the picture of Homecoming I remember both in high school and university. That is the picture that is picturesque. The one we want to continue believing exists. The veil is smooth as silk. Not too sheer, not too opaque. Thin enough to see what's beneath the surface, yet thick enough to hide it, unless you look closely.

Now, let's pierce the veil a bit more. If you look closely, you'll see that what we, albeit unintentionally, revered within those

*woven*

games and celebrations was masculinity, the divinity and toxicity. The sociocultural dichotomy of diverse cultures mingling together, the "playful" mimicking, mocking, and "jokes" that stung ever so slightly but that we laughed off because that was the "cool" thing to do. Thankfully, we have television shows such as *Thirteen Reasons Why, Never Have I Ever, Younger*, and more recently, *Big Little Lies, Little Fires Everywhere, Bridgerton, Sex/Life* that talk about the gravity. Of course, as teens, we didn't clue into the outdated patriarchal ideals that permeate everything we do within society—how we dress, how we speak, how we think, what we allow ourselves to do, what we allow ourselves to step into. The relationships we go on to have with friends and lovers, the academic disciplines we choose to pursue, or even the choice to go be a free spirit who simply lives a life that feels aligned, inside out. Some of us may have an idea, some of us lived through these experiences firsthand, and some of us witnessed others around us live it and breathe it, but we didn't quite know what to say, how to respond, or how to hold space.

And over the course of the last few years, that tide has begun to change. That reckoning is upon each of us, and it is up to each of us to rise into our personal power and reclaim what was once suppressed. Reclaim who we are at our core. It is up to us to stand within our personal power and not live by circumstance alone.

## June 5, 2021.

Today, I woke from the longest afternoon nap. This nap was unlike any other; though fast asleep, I felt awake on a cellular level. I felt like I stepped into an alternate dimension altogether. You're probably reading these words, thinking that I've now grown ten heads and am a bit nuts. Heck, it doesn't quite make sense to me just yet. But in this dimension, I had a familiar "knowing" appear. Like I had been here before. I felt like I had walked these steps before. This journey and voyage weren't new to me. I had these codes, language, memories of myself, old revelations revealed to me. About my lifetimes past and present. About sisterhood, sovereignty, wild woman, a whole other lifetime. And through it all, I felt the deep ache in my heart, my throat and my eyes. Every part of me burned—my throat felt like it had lumps of coal blocking it, my womb felt like something had been ripped out from it, and my eyes burned with salty tears that knew no bounds. An ache for love, home, freedom.

I've had really vivid dreams and visualizations before, but nothing quite like this experience. This felt like an awakening, this felt like a remembering, a homecoming. Like I was finally ready to receive that which has been within me all along. The visions kept coming so quickly, bubbling up to the surface in waves that would not stop crashing. I was walking along the ocean side. And all around me there were mountains, mountains that had been

*woven*

eroded, weathered, corroded by the elements, but they still stood strong and majestic in their glory, their grace, and their grit and resilience for all the world to admire. And I felt like we, too, are just like strong and majestic mountains. Our hearts and beings broken, corroded, climbed, celebrated, and more. And still, we stand. Still, we persist.

I felt like I've been here before. I felt desire in my womb, I felt desire and longing in my heart, along with a slow, burning ache. An ache that hurts the moment I think of pleasure. An ache that hurts the moment I think of love. Followed by a sense of familiarity, a sense of knowing. A sense of grace and holy water washing over me, a sense of forgiveness, a sense of calm. And then in another split second, anger. Anger like I'd never felt before. Anger for letting them use me, anger for letting them drink at my altar. Anger at letting them take from me. Anger for giving away my power with every lash, with every bruise, with every assault, with every word. Pure, sacred anger. And slowly, that anger transformed into shudders and tears. A longing for home, a longing to belong in my skin, in my body, whole divine, feminine, fierce. Me, Seer, Goddess, Creatrix, Maiden, Mother, Wise Woman, Storyteller, Portal. I saw them—all the lovers, even the ones who assaulted me. I saw them in a row. I saw my ancestors; I saw the women in my lineage. I saw their brown skin toiling in the fields. I saw them burning. I saw them getting beaten and bruised. I saw them going through the same cycles. I saw these wounds repeating. *Why her? How can she have this? Why does she get to have her children? Why not me? Why can't you be a good mother; a good girl?* And I'm transported back to the shore, back to the beach where I lie in the sand, tears streaming down my face. I lie there ready to receive, and I do. And so it is.

It all came flooding back to me, this language, this revelation, this knowing. The seer within me, the warrioress within me. My body carries the wounds of the generations before me. My womb carries the imprint of the generations that came before me. My heart carries the ache and the longing for home. And safety. And in a moment, I'm transported back to myself, to my very earthly body.

I don't know what that was. All I know is that I had walked this path before, I have been here before, and I will make it through and I will be okay and that I am here to make an impact, to shift timelines. And so are you. I am here to awaken and ignite. I am here to stop them from drinking at the altar of my, and our, desires. I am here to honor our desires to show you that you can honor who you are and go first and go forth. I am here to serve, lead, and heal myself and every single person who desires what I have to offer. What we have to offer. No longer do we let them plunder us, no longer do we let them loot us, no longer do we let them take, take, and take from us, sometimes through the smell of our skin, sometimes through the smell of our essence, sometimes by penetrating us deep, sometimes by ravaging us. No longer do we let them just take that from us. We hold our power and our magnetism, we hold our desires, we hold our Goddess, we hug our inner child, and we nurture her and come home to her, over and over again. We go forth from there and we lead, and so it is.

I woke up crying at 8:00 tonight, tears streaming down my face, my womb feeling heavy and light, my heart feeling the pain and celebrations of lifetimes. My son continued to stare at me with growing concern as he hugged me tight and touched my face. "Mama, are you okay? Are you sad?" he asks me, worried that I might just attempt to take my own life again. "No, sweetheart, I am okay. Mommy just remembered who she's always been."

# Oh, Fiery Warrioress Kali

Soften.

Heal.

Strengthen.

Grow.

These whispers now roar.

These aches can no longer be repressed.

This voice will no longer be suppressed.

Silent. Meek. Apologetic.

No longer be suppressed to appease YOU.

To appease your mold.

To appease your comfort.

To be constrained in these chains.

To be shackled like a wounded bird.


Awaken my love, awaken.

Let your fury come forth.

Let your Kali come forth.

No longer will she yield out of force.

She will only surrender in faith.

No longer will she be walked all over.

She will choose who receives these most sacred pieces of her.

No longer will her cup overflow freely with her healing medicine.

She will choose who receives her strength, grace, passion, and magic.


Her energy is not for everyone. Nor is it meant to be shared with everyone.

Her energy is sacred, soul-fulfilling, healing medicine.


Awaken Goddess, awaken.

Stand strong, Warrioress.

Soften that gaze, yet look vigilantly, in faith.

Loosen your shoulders, unlock that jaw.

Stop repressing your words for Them.

*woven*

Unclench those fists, feel that peace in your belly.

Feel that strength in your gut, that calmness in your heart,

That certainty in your being saying, "It's okay, Goddess,

you've always been here. Now you're awake. Welcome

home, beautiful Warrioress. You can lay down your armor.

You can leave behind your cloak."

# Chapter 11

# The Reflecting Water

Dr. Parastoo Boroumand

Dr. Parastoo Boroumand

Dr. Parastoo (Paris) Boroumand is a scientist by training. She completed her Honors Bachelor of Science at the University of Toronto, double majoring in Biochemistry, Human Health and Disease with a minor in Physiology. She then completed her Doctor of Philosophy (PhD) at the Biochemistry department of the University of Toronto, studying the effects of obesity-induced inflammation in myeloid cells of the bone marrow. She has fifteen publications from her own and collaborative research projects. She was the recipient of $116,310 in competitive awards and grants for her research and various presentations. During her studies, she developed a graduate level course, Collaborative Science: Student Centered Interdisciplinary Studies, aimed to amalgamate multi-departmental learning and collaboration.

She currently works as a postdoctoral fellow at the SickKids Research Institute and as a medical editor at Klick Health. She is also the founder of Women in Science Society that supports working mothers through hardships of parenthood and their postpartum return to work in research and clinical practice. Furthermore, she is the founder of the nonprofit organization CanadianLove that recruits investors, helpers, and distributors for the annual Acts of Kindness events. Each year, CanadianLove donates food, clothing, and health supplies to the local and international homeless communities, shelters, and health clinics. She also dabbles in the world of business with her start-up company. She lives in Toronto, Ontario, with her husband, Richard Cheng, and their son, Elias.

🅾 @thescientistmom

in Parastoo Boroumand

"To be a bird free to fly and sit atop a tree. But could she fly so high if she had no wings?"

# The Reflecting Water

*So often in life, things that you regard as an impediment turn out to be great, good fortune.*
-Ruth Bader Ginsburg

My given name is Parastoo but I go by Paris, and more recently by Dr. Paris. I wear many hats: a scientist, a course coordinator at the University of Toronto, a postdoctoral fellow at the SickKids Research Institute, a medical editor at Klick Health, an author, a businesswoman working on a start-up company, and the founder of both the nonprofit charity organization CanadianLove and the Women in Science Society. Yet, despite these accomplishments, my most treasured titles include daughter, wife, and closest to my heart, Mom.

I started by sharing my name because I believe, as obvious as it may sound, it is the one word that portrays me the best. It is the first word carefully chosen for me, and over time, it is natural to self-identify with not only the name but also its meaning. Parastoo is a Persian name meaning *lovebird*. *"To be a bird free to fly and sit atop a tree. But could she fly so high if she had no wings?"* Coincidentally, these were the exact words I said minutes prior to finding the inspiration to write this chapter. I have only shared my given name with a handful of close friends, and mostly everyone calls me Paris. Like many bilinguals, I speak my mother tongue from the heart and my learned language from the head. You could say I share my heart with a few and my head with plenty. But I would be foolish to think they were not intertwined, and as the simian crease on my hand indicates, my heart and headlines overlay into one.

While I've shared my name and credentials with you thus far, I haven't shared who I am. You may be surprised to hear that I, too, am still discovering her. Who are we really? Are we divine beings stuck inside mortal capsules? And what is it about us that makes us, us? Is it the capsule or what it contains inside? Consider a glass of water. Most may promptly think, "It is either half empty or half full." I, however, see the water separate from the glass. Our names, our credentials, our possessions are wholly separate from who we are. Yet, we spend our entire existence chasing after decorations for our cups while neglecting the water that sits stagnant inside. After all, like the bird, we need our wings to fly.

*woven*

So, who am I, you ask? I'm no different than you. At its core, we're all one: no gender, no hierarchy, no borders, just humans living through life collecting memories and adding candles to our birthday cakes as life passes by. Living through our versions of ups and downs, sharing laughter and tears with those by our side. And we call those ups and downs our life. Quite literally, without the ups and downs, there would be no life pulsating through our veins. Here, I'll share a few stories about my life. I hope you find that while the height and incline may vary, that your ups and downs are no different than mine. Ultimately, it's the extraordinary experiences, the near-breakable events we survive, and the unremarkable moments that add value to our lives.

## The Extraordinary

I'll start off by sharing an extraordinary story of an unlikely duo of first loves that took place in the midst of the Islamic Revolution and a war in Iran. The story dates back thirty-five years, but it may take you back a century. It's the story about a gold necklace, which I'm wearing right now, of two flying lovebirds with intercepting wings. It was a gift from a twenty-two-year-old boy, who had recently lost his mother to illness and a best friend in the war, given to a sixteen-year-old girl a year after their initial exchange. It's an unlikely but inevitable story because his best friend had unsuccessfully tried to introduce him to a girl living next door.

Little did he know that on May 26, 1986, the boy would be passing a letter to the same girl he was meant to meet. A letter that she ripped up in front of him, like the many she received on her way to school. But this time, she put the pieces back together to read the first words from a man to whom she eventually said, "I do." As you may have guessed, this story belongs to my parents, but I've claimed it as my own, as I have with the necklace, because their choices then have shaped my life today.

The story of their union wasn't quite as brief as I wrote it. In fact, they faced almost six years of obstacles to be together. You see, my grandfather was a wrestling champion in Iran, and if it were up to him, no man was good enough or up to par for his daughters. It didn't help that he held religious and traditional values that often got in the way. For many years, all they heard were NOs from the family:

"No, your older sister is to be married first."

"No, you need to finish your education first."

"No, he doesn't meet our expectations of a son-in-law."

"No, your father will choose your suitor."

They fought against reason after reason of why they shouldn't be together, tooth and nail. Finally, their persistence prevailed. They were both accepted in the country's top universities that happened to be away from home. They got married, and her father agreed to allow them to move in together during their studies. For the

*woven*

first time, they were a unit. Husband and wife, yet on some levels, still strangers, strangers because boys and girls weren't allowed to freely speak and hang out. At times, their only communications were handwritten letters left on the windowsill to be replaced with another . . . their version of today's texting.

You may ask, when do I appear in this story? Well, probably at the worst time. They hadn't graduated yet nor were they quite prepared for how their lives were about to change. My father worked two jobs while going to school, and my mother aligned her classes to when they had childcare. Life wasn't easy, but they made it work. They graduated, became successful professionals in their respective fields and began building a beautiful life for their family. Except that their "happily ever after story" was unfolding in the backdrop of contemporaneous insults to their country. I can't pinpoint the moment that it happened, but facing the hardship of raising a daughter in a country devoid of a prosperous future drove them to make the difficult decision to immigrate somewhere with more promises. After all, you wouldn't leave your home unless home chased you away. But the challenges didn't end there. As any immigrant family knows well, immigration is a process of rebuilding life from scratch. Starting over, longing to make a foreign land your new home. Still, my parents always say, struggling on this side of Earth was worth the life we have today.

I chose this story because it exemplifies many values I hold dear. I watched my parents give up their comfortable life in Iran and take on challenges of immigration to Canada, rebuild our life, and endure the isolation from loved ones for so long. My front-row seat to their unlikely story normalized their hard work, their dedication, and the chasing of their goals despite hearing a herd of NOs. From a young age, they taught me to always evaluate my world, to recreate the life I want, and to dream big. Albeit the most important lesson I learned of all was that it's normal to find love in the most unlikely places, like in the middle of war.

## The Near-Breakable

Remember and rebuild, but never regret the parts of you that were lost in any tragic story. Retain who you were before it happened. Appreciate who you were through it. Project your voice after it happened. End the cycle of silence. Memories of her pop into my head from time to time. A naïve young girl living life, oblivious to the concept of time. Doing what was expected while a part of her wanted to escape. It was fun until it wasn't. Like a caged bird held captive, she laid there, staring into space, waiting for the moment she would be free to fly away.

A bed is an unexpected place where so much of life takes place: births, deaths, acts of love and hate. In this near-breakable story, I lost a part of me because someone couldn't bear losing me. Their failed strategy to keep me was a robbery of a part of me. It led to a clandestine conception deprived of fruition. An ignition of a fire inside me that was never allowed to erupt, and I was left spreading the ashes throughout my life. As strange as it may sound, and while I never wish this on anyone, I can't picture myself without it. I choose every day to live a life I love, and if I had the choice again, I would pass on a life that I couldn't bear to love.

Poised yet dejected, the daily motions of my life resumed within the same hour. A loss is a sobering phenomenon that makes us reevaluate what we hold dear. But a loss in silence is a turmoil of buried emotions. It broke me to not say good-bye to someone who didn't have the words to say hi. Yet, I wore a smile and carried on. I write about it today because while I value my anonymity, I think some stories can't go unwritten. Often, it's the untold stories that have the most ears to fill. In this case, strength arose from my darkest places. Somehow, I am better endowed from it; I love deeper, I forgive sooner, and I appreciate everything I have to hold dear. I've learned that life and death are not in dichotomy. Instead, death is a part of life and not its greatest tragedy.

Esoteric as these words may read, it is very much me—hiding my pain behind elegant words here and behind my stirring accomplishments out in the world. Shortly after this story took place, I reprioritized my life and the people in it. It is easy to get caught up in life and forget how you got there. So, I chose, and still choose every day, to not be a passive participant in my own life but instead to be the driver in the direction it leads. I choose to be the positive change I want to see in the world, to be the unheard voice spoken, and to be the unstoppable force leaving an imprint to last longer than my life—commemorating that no foot is ever too small to leave a mark.

## The Unremarkable

This story takes place in the middle of a lot of seemingly remarkable things. It was the beginning of 2020 when I had just started writing my doctoral dissertation. It was five years in the making, and I was very proud to complete this degree in a top research lab with fifteen publications under my belt. Even more remarkable was that I completed this degree at the same time as my peers, while getting married and having a child. As we call it, balancing life. You can likely guess what happened next. The COVID-19 pandemic hit, and life changed as we knew it then. How I happily rushed to work from home, giving everything up. We all thought it would be temporary. Even my nonprofit organization, Canadian-Love, raised money to provide personal protective equipment to twenty health clinics and to the homeless community—hoping it would make an impact to help us all resume normalcy. Little did we know that it wasn't temporary. And here I am a year later, writing this chapter alone by the water, as I no longer can stay put in my home, a flying bird seeking shelter away from the storm.

Without childcare and with so much on my plate, my goals no longer seemed within reach. I no longer felt like an unstoppable, strong woman in science, working to achieve more than my peers. "The scientist mom," as I was called, felt for the first time at a disadvantage for being a mom. It seemed the only times I had for work were overnights, so I pulled all-nighters to get "some" of my work done. Still, the months went on, the pages of the calendar turned, and my prospective doctoral defense date passed me by. I felt stationary, like a failure, and I could not accept postponing my degree. I devised what I called my "Freedom Plan," and with the help of my support system, I made the impossible a possibility. I was going to defend at the end of 2020, even if my life depended on it. And at times, it really felt like my life depended on it.

I call this story "the unremarkable" because while I achieved my hard-pressed academic goals, it was at the cost of losing a lot of precious moments that at the time I deemed unremarkable. As a breastfeeding mom, I constantly battled mom guilt for spending time away, for not being there to give my son a good-night kiss, for skipping feedings—and it didn't help that my breasts were in pain while staying away. I confronted mom guilt with thoughts that "He won't remember that I'm not there" and that "He is in good hands." The constant reminders of my absence were hearing my son's laughter in the background when I called to check up on him and seeing pictures and videos of him without me there. But if I am being honest, I also felt guilt for not being present, even when I was there. Still, I was so proud of his independence.

One night, I got home early enough to put him to sleep. He refused to go in his crib and wanted to lie down on the floor with me. I hugged my two-year-old boy, and I asked if he was happy. With his little voice, he said, "Happy Mommy home." It wasn't lost on me that life was passing me by in all these unremarkable moments, moments that I would give everything to keep. In trying to make the most of my day, I was missing out on the day-to-day. It has now been six months since my doctoral defense. I'm proud of what I've accomplished, but when I think back to my "big day," the first thing I remember is that I killed a bug on my desk in between my Senate Oral Defense and my examining committee's question period. Funny how the simplest moments are the ones that stay.

I chose not to give this chapter a happy ending because to me, endings are never happy. Life goes on and we move on from all that imprinted us, remembering we are separate from it all. We are the water in the glass: separate from the titles we carry, the obligations and responsibilities we shoulder, and the roles we play every day. We aren't our achievements, we aren't our problems, we aren't our moments of happy or sad. So, who am I, you ask? I am the water in my glass, grateful to be held from dispersing. And as Marty Rubin once said, "Water is always deeper than what it reflects." While I am held, I choose to reflect on my unfolding story. I choose

*woven*

to learn from those around me and from the moments that found me. I choose to count my life's blessings in all its extraordinary, near-breakable, and unremarkable glory.

# Chapter 12

## 3:30 a.m.

Amy Syed

*Amy Syed*

Amy Syed (she/her) is a Coach, Speaker, Author, Registered Kinesiologist/Rehab Professional, and Cybersecurity Professional. She is a serial entrepreneur who believes significant impact can be made through intentional business concepts that foster inclusion, resilience, and sustainability. She teaches these concepts to budding entrepreneurs and career-driven professionals. She is the founder and CEO of FindyourHCP.com and president of Amy Syed Enterprises Inc. Amy has been nominated as Entrepreneur of the Year by RBC and Women of Influence and has been recognized for her contributions by BMO Women, Ella at York, and Scotiabank Women's Initiative. Amy is the host of the podcast, *Calm After the Storm*. Amy is a humanist and an advocate for the Global protection and annihilation of violence against women and children. Amy is a Canadian who is headquartered in Vaughan, Ontario.

🌐 amysyed.ca

📷 @amy.syed

I dedicate this chapter to my father who was with me for a short time in my life but left an impact that has shaped who I am today. I dedicate this to all the children of grief who make sense of loss at a young age and live with the scars to heal for eternity. I also dedicate this to my sisters, Mehvish and Mehreen, who felt the same pain of loss as I did in their unique ways and live to share the beauty of their learnings with the world.

"The truth is not for the weary or for those that love shroud. It's for me, for the people of the sun, the people of the pain. The struggle is not in seeing the truth but accepting it. Making the impact to make the change, take the road less traveled."

# 3:30 a.m.

*When you are lonely and sick of Heart,*
*Go the friends we know.*
*And bury your sorrows in doing good deeds;*
*Miss me, but let me go!*
–Anonymous (Toronto Police Services) in loving memory of Saeed Ahmed Syed

*In the depths of the darkness, I always saw light*

*Like a secret only I knew, a truth, a want.*

*So, I live this life that is etched in my mind and soul*

*Where the truths come to me at 3:30 a.m.*

*When the world is asleep, but my soul stirs me awake.*

*To show me the path I am meant to see*

*The truth is not for the weary or for those that love shroud.*

*It's for me, for the people of the sun, the people of the pain*

*The struggle is not in seeing the truth but accepting it*
*Making the impact to make the change, take the road less*
*traveled.*
*So, when you are astray, you are feeling the melancholy of*
*life*
*Turn to that moment, the truth as it comes to you and know*
*Take solace in knowing of who you are and who you are*
*meant to be*
*Let the truth free.*

I sat staring at the TV.

It was 3:00 a.m.

I had become accustomed to the pangs of panic and the ensuing self-talk to repress the voices in my head. On the other side of the wall, I could hear the oxygen machine and a faint moan every few breaths; I didn't think a lot about it anymore. I stopped thinking about the pain that was being felt to breathe, to move, to be. I continued to stare at the TV with a sense of numbness that had become my daily life.

It took me a few minutes to realize I was watching this movie that was absolutely devastating. It was about a woman who loses her husband to cancer. They documented his life for his children

*woven*

and showcased glints of hope, beauty, bright lights, and eloquence alongside his journey and passing. I became enthralled in the rapture for a moment, wishing that I could experience the same in my real-life situation. I thought, *Wow, how beautiful.* The cultural parallel between the movie and my life was a divergent one. I was experiencing my father dying the way I was being told to experience it. A cross between South Asian culture, Islamic religion, and through the eyes of my grandparents and relatives. I, personally, didn't want to care about all of that. I wanted to be free, much like I had wanted to be free for many years.

My dad had been dying for a while. He was diagnosed with cancer while I was still in my last year of high school and when my little sister was only eleven. He was a best friend, a father who behaved like a mother when he needed to. His love was so pure, it made our lives feel like our biggest problems were getting a good grade in chemistry and asking to go to the school dance. I had never imagined him dying as my reality. So, I trudged on. To just deal with it. But as I watched this movie, I felt a pang of jealousy. The jealousy was embedded in rage. *Why couldn't my dad feel less pain? Why couldn't we talk about it all? Why couldn't I just tell him that it's going to be okay and that he can go?*

The days turned into nights, nights back to other days. The pain of watching him die was so excruciating that I turned to distractions to cope. Working, socializing, and trying to build the life somebody would want at the age of nineteen. With the terrible secret of what was happening at home, I was wrought with guilt all the time, often wondering when the pain would subside to allow for existence, the old existence I had known.

I grew up Canadian first, South Asian second. Born in Toronto and raised in Richmond Hill, a suburb, I lived a life of privilege and experienced parts of both the Canadian and South Asian experience. The value of self-sacrifice and self-martyrdom was woven into me from a young age. It was natural to be self-sacrificing for your family and your immediate community before you thought of yourself. I lived this lifestyle to the best of my ability, but it was such a heavy task that I often crumbled in silence.

What people do not know is that the clash between the heritage of your parents and your own heritage is real. The times we see ourselves as different or the "other" are because we were told by people that the standard is to be like the general population. Although we see racialized and diverse folk in our day-to-day interactions, the media and my experience were reaffirmed every time I saw a blonde-haired, blue-eyed actress, model, and friend. Things just seemed easier for them. They seemed succinct with the way life was supposed to be. There was no pressure to understand others, no embarrassment when they walked down the street with their grandmother. I was mortified with my nani (maternal grandmother)—who also became a Canadian citizen in her lifetime—who

*woven*

wore *shalwar kameez*, traditional Pakistani clothes outside of the house. This way of life felt like a struggle. It felt like it was out of the ordinary, and in my generation, for me at least, ordinary is what I was striving for. So, when I came to realize and embrace the beauty of my culture, the beauty of my life, the beauty of existence, it felt like it was too late. Experiencing my father's cancer diagnosis was a horror reel that still plays in my mind today—twenty-two years later. It was so unjustified, and it felt so wrong. I kept feeling like I would wake up and it would all be a bad dream.

Cancer is a strange disease. It takes parts of you slowly, slowly, inch by inch. It consumes your insides. It surfaces in the heart-breaking loss of dignity. I watched my father wither from the man he once was. The man who was a sergeant with the Toronto Police Services. The man who was one of the founding members of the "Ethnic Relations" unit, now known as Community Relations. He always told us that culture and religion do not define us as anomalies but rather the diversity in our existence is what brings us together. *Did it?* I refer back to all the things he used to say to me, the noble and empathetic way of living. To feel for others, to celebrate other holidays and religious beliefs. To respect other cultures in times of happiness and in times of sorrow. His strength in leadership, his strength in community, and his amazing ability to lift up anybody with whom he spoke. They continue to haunt me and mesmerize me, even twenty-two years later, especially as I witness the ever-changing sociocultural landscape of this country I call home.

I am painfully aware of all the sacrifices that were made for me to exist on this land today. The plight of my ancestors who, because of the color of their skin, because of their origins, have migrated from one place to another. In reflection, twenty-two years after the death of my father, I am left with the remnants of my past. I can either honor them and pay homage to them while deepening my understanding, or I can hide away from them. I choose to honor and embrace these fragments of my past that give me solace in knowing that through the struggles and sacrifices of my ancestors, my people have been through world wars, mass migrations, and displacements. They have seen the unthinkable. Our diaspora is fragmented yet rooted in a time capsule—many embracing the Canadian way of life while still clinging on to the fragments of culture, heritage, language, and norms they remember. Fragments that have been embedded within them from generation to generation. Perhaps that is what prepared me for what I have seen in my life. I do know that the strength within me as a child, the understanding and empathy of others, came to a boiling point when I witnessed my father's death.

I remember the wailing, the difficulty I had over letting him go. I had been at work. I had this intuitive feeling that something was amiss and called home. I rushed home because they said it was coming to an end. When I entered the home, there it was. Death hung in the air like a long-lost relative who finally found our doorstep. When I entered the room, my father looked like a baby, heaving slow breaths methodically. This gurgle, from what I learned later was a death rattle, was a clear indicator his time on Earth was now nearing its end. We stood together, my sisters and I, beside him. I held his head in my hands.

What happened next shaped my life forever. It reminds me every day that the proof of life and death are for the living. That we can, in a moment, learn infinite wisdom, simply by being present. The room we were gathered in became so small, and the focus on the last breaths he had left to give revealed the world I did not know. I was humbled. I was suddenly so aware that there is so much more to a person and their life than we can comprehend. There was a sense of peace hidden within the bittersweet feeling of letting go. And then there was the chaos of pain and the wailing and mourning that accompanied it. The wailing still rings in my ears when I learn of somebody's death. The wailing caged me for life. I looked at the time; it was 3:30 a.m. For a moment, time came to a standstill. A release. At the young age of twenty, I understood so much and so little at the very same time. I was forever changed. I saw the secret to life.

At that moment, despite the loud wailing that was laced with pain and sadness, I could hear my heart pounding, louder, more resonant than anything else. I could no longer feel his heartbeat. The warmth felt like it was slowly leaving his body as I laid his head on the pillow. I've remembered that moment every day for the last twenty-two years. At first it felt like pain and sadness, but now it feels empowering to have lived that intimate moment. I used to think that people who are present in a room with someone who dies should die with the person. Metaphorically speaking. But I soon realized that it was like a truth that was meant to be told, an intimate detail not everyone will experience in this life. A privilege.

So, when I reflect on the experiences of my life, as the other in a world where I belong and do not belong at the very same time, I remember my father's words to me: "Life is for the living. To be strong, to carry on, and to make an impact. Because after you're gone, you will not be remembered unless you leave that legacy in your everyday relationships and in every single time you touch someone's heart."

In realization and gratitude of these words, I have experienced profound truths and have lived to now tell them. Will you join me? Will you take the first step toward shaping your legacy, owning your truth and sharing it, embracing the fragments and shreds that are so intricately sewn together to create the beautiful kaleidoscopic lens that is your life?

# Chapter 13

# Tears of Joy

Jennifer De Rossi

*Jennifer De Rossi*

Jennifer De Rossi is a creative soul who is inspired by the deep complexities of life as it flows through everything and everyone. She is a mixed-media artist and holds several certifications including Reiki master, yoga and meditation teacher, and spiritual coach. As a new mother, at the age of thirty-one, she was diagnosed with breast cancer and entered her dark night of the soul — an event that she now believes was the greatest blessing and awakening of her life thus far. Embarking on her healing journey, Jennifer quickly became fascinated by the world of holistic wellness, quantum physics, and spirituality. Through these practices, Jennifer was able to heal herself from a lifetime of emotional blocks and free herself from the limiting beliefs that kept her trapped in a cycle of dis-ease. Along this path, she grew to love the potent healing power of attending women's circles.

Inspired to create more connection, she teamed up with her best friend, Ellie, and Moonstone Collective was born. Hosting and facilitating events, retreats, soul circles, and personal growth courses, this community of like-minded souls cultivates connection and sacred space on the journey to self-discovery, holistic wellness, and inspired living.

This life is filled with infinite possibilities, stretching out to the furthest corners of the universe. Jennifer's mission is to help others choose love over fear and to expand our awareness of the beauty, wonder, and inspiration available to us — no matter the circumstances.

🌐 moonstonecollective.ca

📷 @jenniferderossi

📷 @moonstonecollectivewellness

This offering is dedicated to my daughter, Gioia. Thank you for choosing this life, for being our support system, and for the constant reminder that joy is always available to us. May you always remember the magic that is within you, through all of life's moments—both the aching and the inspiring.

"Why wait for pain to ignite change when we can intentionally seek inspiration to do the same?"

# Tears of Joy

*Everything you can imagine is real.*
-Pablo Picasso

There is a Japanese theory of change that demonstrates how every period of extreme transformation or awakening comes from either a Kensho or Satori moment.

Kensho moments are moments of growth as the result of temporary pain: an illness, a loss, the ending of a relationship, or anything that helps push you to want to make a change because you realize you aren't happy with your current reality.

Satori moments are moments of growth as a result of actively pursuing knowledge or being inspired. They gently push us to our next level of consciousness, whereas Kensho moments are more of a shove.

We are spiritual beings having a human experience, and part of that experience is to learn lessons and evolve. We are meant to journey closer to our soul. But if we fail to shift and change, if we become stagnant, the Universe intervenes to help us in whatever way it can.

But why wait for pain to ignite change when we can intentionally seek inspiration to do the same? By doing so, when pain inevitably happens, we are then much more equipped with the right tools to move through it.

As it turns out, pain was what happened as a result of me not seeking inspiration. It forced me to look within. To take care of me, first. And then, it reminded me of the inspiration that is all around me. It was only when I began tapping inward that I started silencing the noise surrounding me and listening to my own inner voice. It was only with the ticking clock that I felt the urgency to make a change. To live life on purpose, and to declare that I was done listening to anyone but myself. To trust my beliefs and my body. To make it all just a part of my colorful story.

Over time, I've learned to seek the Satori moments. I live for learning and growth. I stretch my mind to the far corners of my current paradigm until I discover an opening to the next one. I free-fall into new beginnings instead of holding myself back. This wasn't always the case, however.

*woven*

## Beginnings

Pain and inspiration, I find, are often intertwined. They coexist together. The greatest ideas, art masterpieces, creative endeavors, and healing modalities are often born out of a desire to find inspiration within deep, dark moments. To find new beginnings when it seems like your life is abruptly ending, literally and metaphorically.

I love beginnings. In fact, I consider myself to be somewhat of a *beginning connoisseur*. I love the thought of a new idea, the inspiration that comes to me in one fell swoop, then builds upon itself, taking shape and gaining momentum. I love the flutter and excitement about it all. I love dreaming up possibilities. I love to begin. And I'm not afraid to begin again.

For me, a new beginning, in many instances, used to mean the failed attempt of something else. The guilt of not following through. My ego would drive me to focus on the excitement of the new to distract me from the ending of the old, while my subconscious would wire together the belief that I wasn't good enough, setting me up for the inevitable and detrimental cycle yet again. Each time, I'd discard the idea into the proverbial pit of failure. Like a broken lamp, tossed away before checking if all that was needed was a new bulb. And the more lamps I'd cast off, the heavier the reminder became. The stronger the belief that I was not worthy. I was so distracted from the pressure to *do* that I overlooked how to *be*.

Eventually, the thought of starting again became unbearable. So, I stopped.

I stopped the inspiration before it could sweep me off my feet with excitement. I set aside my passions and decided it was time to grow up and start living in the real world. In doing so, I somehow stopped living my truth, and I stopped owning my desires.

Shortly after, I succumbed to the pressure of the great divide—the moment in life where you are faced with risking it all and doing what you love or taking the safe route. So, I got a steady job, told myself *I'd work hard enough to earn the right to follow my dreams and create the life I wanted.* I didn't think I deserved it just yet.

I explored every creative avenue I could, taking jobs and starting side hustles as a wardrobe stylist, a closet organizer, an event planner, an event designer, and event installation artist.

There it was again, the starting . . . drifting . . . the always something new—moving from one creative job to the next without any real sense of purpose. Eventually, I decided perhaps my purpose was simply to be a mother. I got married and had a daughter, Gioia. *Ah, this must be it.* The entire Universe was cradled in my arms, and she was all that mattered. I had a husband who made enough to support us financially, and I was going to be the best wife and mother I could be.

For the first time, *this* was a job I didn't want to resign from. It was clear that I had fulfilled a core purpose. What I did not yet

*woven*

realize though, was that I had more purpose to be discovered.

It didn't take long before I began getting nudges to start again. After the initial nights of little-to-no sleep fell into somewhat of a routine, it started happening again.

Motherhood was (and is) not easy, but I was in it. And while I love my daughter more than anything, I still felt this inner calling to do more with my life. I felt the pressure to begin again building within me, its vast current of energy just below the surface.

The reality was that I was overlooking a deep inner truth. A whisper from my soul trying its best to get my attention until it grew so loud that I could no longer ignore it.

## Dark Night of the Soul

My best friend was getting married in Mexico. I was so excited to get away. I had had a lovely girl give me an organic tan during my pregnancy and thought it would be a perfect option for this trip. So, I set up the appointment for two days before we left.

I began to undress, and the girl handed me the nipple covers I had requested since I was still breastfeeding. When I got to my right side, I felt a hard mass that hadn't been there before. My stomach immediately dropped, and just as I had a flash of the unthinkable, the girl plugged in her machine and the power went out.

We had used the exact same outlet the last time I had a spray tan, and nothing had changed since then. *Or had everything changed?*

Talk about a major sign from the Universe—as if to confirm my worst thoughts at that moment. The pathetic fallacy could not have been more exact. *Was my world about to go dark?*

## The "C" Word

I will never forget the moment my oncologist entered the diagnosis room. My husband and daughter were with me. I was taken aback, but a large part of me felt relieved that I finally had an answer, that I finally had an excuse to make a change in my life. Saying it out loud now sounds crazy, I know. But the reality is that I had felt "off" for so long and couldn't explain why to anyone. I felt like I needed permission from someone, anyone, to simply be there for myself. To be myself.

After the initial breakdown of tears, I pulled myself together enough to review my options. I had heard of others' experiences in this moment, but mine wasn't like anything I had read about. It was like I already knew what I had to do. I wiped my eyes dry. I listened to my options, and my doctor was kind enough to write them out with little diagrams beside each one. Instinctively, I already knew what my choice would be.

I asked her what I needed to be doing, not doing, eating, and anything else I could think of. I wanted to do whatever I could to support my health. The prescribed series of medical interventions were as follows:

- Egg Retrieval
- Surgery
- Chemo
- Possible Radiation
- Hormone Suppressant for ten years

During this process, I spent a lot of time in waiting rooms, reading and doing research. One day, it hit me. What if I decided not to?

I decided to have the surgery but put chemotherapy on the back burner momentarily so I could heal. I had eight weeks to decide. I underwent a full double mastectomy, with reconstruction, and what happened during those eight weeks of recovery was nothing short of a miracle.

I kept hearing story after story about women who chose not to do chemotherapy, and I began to feel a massive weight lifting off me, as I discovered an even more powerful "C" word.

## Choice

Leading up to my surgery, and during recovery, I had to make a choice. A choice that, as crazy as it sounds, I didn't think I was allowed to make at first.

When my surgical oncologist went through my options the day of my diagnosis, I did not hear, "Have the surgery, but then change your lifestyle habits and skip the drugs." Or even, "Do none of the above."

I am not claiming that the provided choices were wrong, I just didn't realize others existed. I had never questioned authority, and I avoided all forms of confrontation. But what I hadn't realized was that in doing so, I was suppressing my truth. I wasn't asking myself, or my body, for the answers. I was just blindly going along with what the outer world told me to do, forfeiting my power over and over again.

The moment this new option entered my awareness, and I began to align with it, things changed.

## The Healing Power of the Collective

I never realized how being vulnerable could help and inspire others while simultaneously healing myself. I first decided to share my story about the day of my surgery when I came home from the hospital. Perhaps it was the remnants of strong medication, or maybe it was divine intervention—a nudge to take this first step on the journey to my purpose. It also just so happened to be International Women's Day.

The hours that followed my social media post were magical. People from all over the world were sharing my story and, more importantly, opening up about their own struggles. They said that my message was encouraging, and it helped put things in perspective. I had, unknowingly, opened a portal for women to begin using their voices, to share the difficulties of life behind the highlight reel we have all grown accustomed to, and to feel connected to one another, even if only by a thread of hope.

I found my purpose in one word—inspiration. I had found a Satori moment. Every time I saw that word, every time someone referred to me as "inspiring," I anchored into it, allowing it to send loving vibrations right to my heart and to fill my energetic field with its power. I credit the response and loving energy that I received that day to my incredible and quick recovery. I never had to take significant pain medication, and my surgical oncologist was floored with how easily and smoothly my recovery went.

Three weeks after my surgery, I received the incredible news that my lymph nodes had come back clear. I screamed out of pure excitement and relief. As my surgical oncologist began to examine my scars, she said, "Wow, you're healing so quickly. Whatever you're doing, keep doing it." I addressed a concern I had about my right arm, as it was not able to stretch out completely or extend up over ninety degrees. I was told it most likely would not get back to normal for several months, as the removal of my sentinel lymph nodes had caused an adverse reaction called axillary web syndrome or "cording."

About a week or so later, I visited an energy worker. She practiced various techniques on me, and when I mentioned my cording, she led me through a breath-work technique, and I repeated the exercise with her a few times. I didn't notice any physical changes in mobility, but I did feel a bit more relaxed. When I got home that evening, I repeated the technique a few times on my own. Still, no change. I was a bit skeptical, but I told myself I'd practice it for a few weeks. After all, it did seem to calm my nervous system.

The next morning, I woke up to discover my arm bent up over my head. There was no pain. I glanced at my arm and brushed the surface of my skin with my fingertips. The cording was gone. The rope-like buildup under my skin had dissolved.

When I shared what had happened with my surgical oncologist, she smiled and said, "Sometimes, things happen that we can't fully explain."

What an understatement. Thus began my journey even deeper down the rabbit hole. I could not crawl out if I tried.

## The Rabbit Hole

Japanese scientist and photographer, Masuru Emoto, was fascinated with water—in particular, it's molecular structure and how it is affected. He applied mental stimuli to water and photographed it using a microscope. The water was measured and photographed before any *intentions* were placed on it. Then, using various intentions and words taped to the outside of the bottles, he would photograph the water again. The molecules in the water droplets that were blessed with positive emotions such as gratitude and love photographed in a beautiful, symmetrical crystal formation. The ones with negative intentions like hurt or anger looked sickly and diseased.

Considering our bodies are made of more than 70 percent water, *could we shape and affect our bodies simply with our intentions?*

The subconscious mind does not know the difference between what is happening in the present reality and what is a memory or imagination, meaning we can co-create our reality however we desire. This mind-bending concept did not feel as new to me as it did familiar—like I was waking up from decades of slumber and recalling my innate wisdom.

In the initial stages of my healing journey, I was on a mission to heal myself. I obsessively read every book, article, or study. I listened to every podcast, audiobook, and meditation. I made changes in my physical life: I started taking herbs and supplements and eating plant-based superfoods and juices, I practiced yoga almost every single day, I had a reverse osmosis water filter installed, I went for acupuncture, I journaled, and I practiced gratitude. I ate, slept, and breathed healing and wellness.

Each day I got rid of what wasn't working and added more of what I thought would work. As I made these changes, something else started to happen. I became paralyzed with fear—fear that I wouldn't do enough to keep the beast away. The more I changed, the longer my list of things I wanted to change or try became.

Then, one morning during my meditation ritual, it happened. A huge release. As it left my body, I suddenly felt lighter.

*I don't need to be healed to be complete. I am good enough as I am, in this moment.*

Accepting this truth sent a rush of compassion to my heart center. I felt the shift happening within me. I sensed my brain rewiring; I breathed even deeper in the moment of clarity. It was time to get to work.

## The Work

I strongly believe that my diagnosis was put in my path to help me to deal with emotions I buried deep down for years and mental habits that were subconsciously formed that were detrimental to my health. It's in darkness that we learn the lessons. Where we feel. We need to break the stigma of feeling emotions as a diagnosis.

When we do the inner work, we choose to face our traumas and emotional blocks head on. To bring them to the surface, through the veil of the subconscious mind, to be healed. We don't judge them, dismiss them, or suppress them, rather we invite them in with confidence, compassion, and faith. We do not try to erase the possibility of feeling fear, anxiety, sorrow, or grief. We are simply better equipped with the tools to help us move through them. And the best part is that as we continue to do the inner work, we make an impact on those around us as well. They feel inspired to be of service to themselves and others, thus creating a ripple effect that expands into the collective, forever changing the shape of humanity in ways we may never fully comprehend or see.

## Defying Statistics

If the doctor sitting across from me was telling me that I should go with recommended treatment based on statistics, then I, too, could argue that I should make a decision on statistics as well.

For example, in a study[1] that looked at 1,500 breast cancer patients, women who increased their fruit and vegetable intake by five servings/day and incorporated moderate exercise thirty minutes a day had a 50 percent reduction in mortality than those who did not. In other words, they lived twice as long.

To me, cancer wasn't and isn't a sentence. It's merely a word. More than that, it is a messenger that helped me tap into the fact that something was out of alignment. The goal is to find that something, work on correcting it, and observe as the body's immune system begins to correct itself back to a healthy state of ease instead of being in perpetual dis-ease.

The choice I made to listen to my intuition was not an easy one. It meant going against everything the authority figures around me were suggesting and recommending. But here's the thing: either way you look at it, I'd be taking a risk. The only thing I could do, in that moment, was tap into the innate system within my body and follow it, while surrendering the rest to the Universe.

Emoto's theory echoed within my mind . . . this was my Kensho and Satori moment intertwined together. I, too, could co-create my reality, regardless of how it played out. I was willing to bet on myself, my body, my health, and take that risk. Because the way I looked at it, statistics could also be defied.

## Co-Creator

In a way, I have always known that I am able to create what I desire. The act of creating, of being in flow is like saying to the Universe, "Hey, I'm leaning in. I am putting my faith in you to deliver whatever is meant to come to me, to emerge and to teach me." It's not having an expectation of what will become of a particular piece or project, rather intending to be open to possibility. It leaves space for magic.

I continue to practice choosing love over fear, even when it is uncomfortable or inconvenient. I want to feel it all, the tough and sticky emotions too. For not only do we feel to heal, we have the dark to contrast the light.

The Universe, or whatever higher power you believe in, is forever conspiring with you to give you exactly what your heart desires. But you have to lean in. You have to surrender in relentless trust. I want you to realize that you no longer need to be at the mercy of any prescribed outcomes, and that it is safe to turn inward and trust your intuition.

I am proud of the choices I've made and continue to make even when they weren't the "right" ones. I made these decisions to live my best life. To be an active participant in my own unfolding. I did not just take the position of a bystander.

Listen, I'm not your guru. I'm not here to tell you what to do, what steps to take, or how to live your life. I'm simply here to inspire you to journey inward until you find your soul. My hope is to shed some light down the path to your center. To be the kindle in your lantern that guides you to your own inner glow. To reassure you that some paths you travel will be darker than others, painful even, but you must keep this flame lit. It will get you out of any situation and lead you home.

When you begin to believe this truth, you start noticing things happening in your current reality that almost seem impossible. Synchronicities happen regularly, and you receive signs and confirmations that reassure you that you are on the right path, so keep going. These are reminders that you are aligning with your soul's path and purpose, and you have nothing to fear.

When the Universe started delivering to me all the abundance I had visualized over the past two years, it came flooding in almost all at once and was even a bit overwhelming. Within about a six-month period, I had landed my first big art commission and held multiple events and retreats online for our community: Moonstone Collective. I had also prelaunched an online coaching program. And to top it off, I landed the final spot for this book.

The day before the first draft of this chapter was due, I was frantically typing away at my computer while my daughter was glued to the iPad. When my husband came home from work, my tears started falling uncontrollably, and I vented to him about how stressed I was and how I didn't know if I could do it all.

Then, I thought back to what I had learned from Masuru Emoto. I decided my tears could mean whatever I intended them to be. "Hey, you're going to do this. Everything will get done, and it will all be amazing," my husband confidently assured me.

In a fragment of a moment, I had shifted the intent within my tears as a healing release that made space for the wonder and joy that was filling my life.

I turned to my husband and replied with conviction,

*"I know it will. These are my tears of joy."*

# Chapter 14

# Social Ceilings and Motherhood Norms

MICHELLE NICOLET

*Michelle Nicolet*

Michelle Nicolet wears many hats, including being a mom to four children. She is a medically released military veteran who climbed to Everest Base Camp and Island Peak, and she participated in the movie *March to the Top* as well as in Wounded Warrior fundraisers by cycling across Europe. Michelle is a recipient of the Queen's Diamond Jubilee Award, and she has served her country for the past thirty-one years in the military, public service, and most recently, with Veteran's Affairs as a Field Nursing Services Officer for Kingston, Ontario. During this time, Michelle suffered injuries from her service and second marriage. These challenges have served to strengthen and fortify her as well as to teach her to continually improve, learn, and evolve. Michelle has a bachelor's degree in nursing from Ottawa University, a certificate in PeriAnesthesia nursing, and she is currently working on her Real Estate license. Michelle loves karate, and she took her youngest to train with her in Japan in 2017. Her kids are her heroes, and her dogs keep her company as she learns how to use her experience and knowledge to help others.

@heartandarmour

@mamamichellern

To my kids, Kane, Zara, Vanja, and Rhys. You kept the smile on my face, gave me strength when I didn't think I had any, and provided me with hope on days when I couldn't find any. Your smiles, your laughter, and your hearts walk with me every day, and I love who you are and who you are becoming. I love you for all the reasons, and I am so thankful for you each and every day. Continue to be you, trust yourself, and live on your terms. Love, Mom, Mum, Mummah, and Mother.

"The Herculean magnetic pull to be true to myself was what drew me to make choices in my life that would continue to keep me tethered to my true self—choices that would continue to shatter every possible limitation we impose on ourselves and allow society to impose on us."

# Social Ceilings and Motherhood Norms

*My mission in life is not merely to survive, but to thrive; and to do so with some passion, some compassion, some humor, and some style.*

–Maya Angelou

After eighteen years of military service, I finally got the call. A nurse had to come off deployment to Afghanistan. This position was what I had trained for, and what I had always wanted to do—serve Canada in a time of war. To say I was excited would be an understatement.

However, at eighteen years into my career, serving was not part of the plan. I was a single parent to three amazing kids, ages four, six, and nine at the time. Two little girls and my oldest, my son. This call was my dream and my nightmare, all rolled into one. How in the heck could I serve my country overseas and at the same time leave my children for a total of seven months?

I had no idea, yet I had forty-eight hours to let my commanding officer know if I would be able to go or not. It was a very heavy decision. *What should I do?* I reached out to my close friends and my mom for advice and support. My mom, who lived in British Columbia, had been such a staunch supporter of everything military and building a career with them that I knew she was in my corner. However, since she too worked, she was unable to do both—work and care for my kids at the same time. Since I joined the Canadian Armed Forces in 1988, I was posted to Eastern Canada and Ontario, and she was never in a position where she could help. This time was no different, her heart hurt for me, she supported me wholeheartedly, but she couldn't help me. My sister had her own family and kids, so there was no help available there either. So, that was it: the near end of my desire to go serve my country. The only other option I had was to have the kids' dad step up to the plate, or I wouldn't be able to go. Logically, that made sense. Emotionally, however, I was torn. *How can I? How can I go even a week without my baby girl telling me she loves me when she sneaks into my bed to snuggle? Oh, God! What in the world do I do?* The tears fell, and they fell hard.

*woven*

When I first joined the Canadian Military, I was seventeen (and a bit) and was more than wanting to do anything scary and dangerous. My stepdad moved us from my hometown of Squamish, BC, to Egmont, BC, and I couldn't wrap my head around the fisherman lifestyle. Everyone in Pender Harbour lived that lifestyle and enjoyed it, but I knew it wasn't for me. So, after graduation, with no money for university, off I went—to be all that I could be. Heck, it looked so exciting. However, that was not part of the plan for me, something I realized over the years. I completed training, got my medic qualification, then once I had a posting and career, I thought, *what's next?* And once again, the girl who buried her nose in a book for so many years thought the next best thing was marriage and kids. At the time, I thought that was my path.

When the Gulf War broke out, a colleague and I were offered the next phase of our medical training a year early. I thought about it and decided that I would take the course and go on the next rotation to the Middle East as a trained medic. That worked out to only 50 percent. I received my qualification, but the war was over and there was no second rotation to the Middle East for me to go on. Subsequently, there were rotations to Somalia and Rwanda. For Somalia, I was stationed in Gagetown, New Brunswick, on a posting with my then-husband and not in a unit that was being tasked with deployment. For Rwanda, at the unit assembly where they announced who the deploying members were, I was informed that my application to become a nursing officer had been accepted. Instead of going to Rwanda, I was off to university to become a nursing officer. Stellar student, check. Beautiful family, check. Marriage breaking down, also check (though this one, I didn't see coming at the time).

So, here I was, eighteen years of service in, single parent to three kids, with an opportunity for a deployment on my plate. It was tempting like a huge juicy steak; however, it was so damn expensive. The decision was huge and probably one of the hardest decisions I've had to make to this date. My kids were (and are) my world. Everything I had done throughout my career had been according to some predesigned plan in my head. I have no idea why I had this plan or why I thought it was the right thing to do, but I had this life template in my head that I seemed to be following to a T. The only thing that was off the plan was the divorce.

When I gave birth to my third child, I realized that my first ex-husband and I were not compatible. He was not a bad person, he was just married to his career first, and the kids and I came second. Our relationship was not at all how those romance novels I buried my head in as a teen portrayed romance, marriage, and family. It was not in my vision. He also was in a unit that deployed quite often, so I had been a solo parent many times, which didn't scare me at all. So, I knew I had to leave that relationship and forge ahead, which I did.

*woven*

Now, I was faced with a decision to leave my kids to serve my country. This situation was not how it was supposed to work, but I know now that the best life lessons come to us when we are faced with growth and challenges. And growth isn't always easy. Nobody will ever know what it feels like except those who have been in similar circumstances.

All the fears of motherhood and expectations flooded my brain:

*Good moms don't leave their kids.*

*Good moms are always there for their children.*

*Good moms don't leave the country for their jobs.*

Yet, another part of me struggled so hard. *Why not? Like seriously, why the eff not?*

My ex was doing his career, seeing his kids every other weekend and sometimes not even then because he would have work obligations, and yet my kids jumped for joy when they saw him, and it did not seem to affect their love for him one iota. He saw them on fun, playful weekends. He was the fun parent. I was more the weekday taskmaster who ran a tight ship by getting them up and ready for school, picking them up, ensuring homework was completed, and getting them to bed on time every single weeknight. In my eyes, it seemed like he had the best of the two worlds. The kids would talk about him like he was so fun, so amazing, and yes, I had pangs of jealousy when I grounded them or sent them to bed early or had to discipline them for something. *Why the double standard? Who wrote these rules? I really wanted to have a cold, hard conversation with this person! Why can't a mother with a career do the same as the father and be respected?*

*Ticktock, ticktock.* I only had forty-eight hours to make my decision and very limited resources to confide in. I discussed the situation with my kids' babysitter (she was the spouse of a military member), and she let me know that she was posted to the same base as my ex and therefore, the kids would have their dad and her—their same babysitter while I was away. Also, my sister was at the same base as my ex.

Wow, it all seemed to be aligning perfectly. I could see the light. I summoned the courage to call my ex. I told him that I had the opportunity to go on an overseas deployment and that I needed him to take the kids for seven months.

I will never forget the words that came next: "Michelle, I can't do that; it will greatly affect my flexibility at work." Wow. I had to let that sink in.

Rage. Anger. And yes, if I'm being honest, jealousy. He had the option to even say these words. I had given up management courses that would further my rank because I didn't want to leave my kids or have the increase in rank mean moving them to another base. Yet, here he was, their father, saying it would affect his flexibility at work? Flashes of running out of work to beat the daycare closing times so that I wouldn't be charged the extra $10 per minute flooded my mind. Flashes of having to get up at 0500 to ensure that I was ready and that packing all lunches and bags for the sitter and school were done before having to be at physical training by 0630. *Wow, what did this unicorn named flexibility actually look like?* Now, don't get me wrong; I loved being the parent and mom, and being the perfect mom was on my to-do list. I just never could complete it with any precision or elegance. I felt like a freight train rushing from station to station, always a second too late and holding a suitcase that had clothes sticking out of it and about to burst open. Yet, he calmly stated that he couldn't risk his flexibility at work. I was gobsmacked.

There, *that* was the reason I was out of the marriage. However, he had gone on two tours since we split and not once did he consider asking me if his being away would make an impact on me in any way. I had no weekends to catch up on cleaning, laundry, sleep, or to just "recharge." Back then, the terms "self-care" and "me time" did not exist like they do today. I had no idea why I always felt exhausted and not "good enough." Nobody talked about their insecurities or misgivings. We kept that shit close to our chest and carried on. We lived like the walking dead, much like living zombies, disconnected from our soul, our desires, what made us feel happy. We felt like we could never make the final cut of "good mom." I would show up to school functions with store-bought cupcakes because there would be absolutely no time to "bake" a homemade cake for so-and-so's birthday at school the next day. Good grief, the perfection mill never stopped. Yes, to say I felt inadequate as a mom would be an understatement. So, to hear this statement from my children's own dad, I was crushed. Again, I was flooded with questions of *Why? Why do dads get this free pass while moms are not given a choice? Why? Who made these rules, and why am I seemingly the only one who feels that they are wrong and unequal?* Screams were wild in my head.

At that juncture, we were separated and not yet divorced. It was amicable by any standard; however, I felt backed against a wall. I let him know that I wanted to earn my money fair and square, but if he continued on this path, I would go for the divorce and pursue my half of his pension as well. I gave him twenty-four hours to let me know his decision.

Being career-driven and financially focused, he decided that he would take the kids for the time I was away.

Okay, hurdle one out of the way. Next up, my two oldest were attending Francophone school. Not just immersion but fully Francophone school. My ex, not knowing any French except "bonjour," told me he would be putting the kids in English school, as he wouldn't be able to understand their homework or any of the notices. I panicked. Kids are most malleable when they are young, and they absorb information and learn at lightning speeds in their own unique way. My youngest was due to start school soon; if

*woven*

she started in English, there would be no way to get her back into the Francophone system.

Again, my brain went into overdrive. *How could this work?* I didn't want my kids who had been in Francophone school since day one to have to try and learn in English on top of being away from their mom. I thought hard. I countered that I would wake up every night while on tour (and on school days) at 3:00 a.m. (4:00 p.m. Ontario time) and translate the work for him.

He agreed. *Oh, my goodness, thank heavens.* One of my personal goals, since my schooling in British Columbia, was to be bilingual. And I knew that when I had kids, I'd give them that gift from the start. Translating their French homework would keep that goal alive. Oh, the fires that stoke the burning hearts of mothers.

By now, my friends were hearing about my deployment. I kept receiving phone calls, one after the other, asking me, "How the heck can you even think about leaving your children? This is wrong. Your children will suffer without your presence." It bothered me, and let me tell you, I cried a lot. Why is it okay for dads to pack up and leave for work but not moms? Can *we as women* not show our kids, families, and the world that *we* are just as capable? That *we, too,* can work and be parents? That *we* love our children and families just as much, but we can also have thriving careers? So many of my military girlfriends didn't have kids. They made a conscious decision to serve their country and then kids didn't fit into the picture. Yet, men married, had kids, and did their deployments all the time. This double standard confused and bothered me.

It brought me back to my childhood when my stepfather would tell me that I couldn't mow the lawn because it was a boy's job. My brain would just about explode every single time I heard those antiquated words. Who made these rules?! Who decided which gender was stronger and more capable and desirable than the other? Or the types of jobs each gender could perform? I remember thinking I wanted that job one day. Hilarious, now, old and crotchety, I realize it isn't a job rather a set of societal standards that only we, the ones who are unhappy with them, can actually shatter. Hail to the glass-ceiling crushers! You are my heroes!

I made my decision. I was going to crush that ceiling. Societal norms and gender norms be damned. I was going to crush that ceiling, serve my country, raise my children, and fulfill my dreams. I would make it work. Done and be damned the naysayers.

The prep work for this mission was anything but easy. My brain hurt, and I physically felt the pangs of heartache at the thought of not seeing my kids every day. However, I also wanted my kids to know that their mom was just as strong as their dad. I wanted my girls to know that love had no boundaries, that you can do whatever you want and still love your family just as much. I hoped and prayed that this lesson would stick. My kids were four, six, and nine, so it may have been a stretch for me to hope for this, but now, looking back, I think maybe it did just that.

My kids, now twenty-six, twenty-three, twenty-one, and fifteen are adventurous. My daughter took a job in Australia and Italy during the summer months of her first year of university and was fearless in her explorations. My son sold everything he owned and moved across the country for his love. My youngest daughter is looking to study in England, and my youngest son has yet to forge his path. Live your dreams, my babies, for we only get one chance at this thing called life. And, yes, you CAN weave adventure, love, career, family—all of it and none of it—whatever the eff you want into the tapestry of your life in whatever fabric you choose and whatever color you choose.

My point from my difficult lesson is that it is our journey. Our path. All the opinions of others fall by the wayside because at the end of the day, we have to feel good in our own skin. I can only stand by my choices. My choice to go on tour didn't sit well with many people. In fact, there were many who looked at me differently for leaving my kids. It was such a societal opposition, and I felt it. When I was asked about my family, I got the odd looks and the questions of "How could you?" I don't feel it was a question of how could I but after holding those kinds of beliefs my entire life, how could I not? How could I not walk the walk if I talked the talk? I believed that women could do anything they wanted, so why would I not follow my own instinct and be true to myself? I felt having my kids see my being true to myself would be the best and most fulfilling lesson. I came home and, unfortunately, many soldiers did not. I got to continue watching my children grow and live. I know I am one of the lucky ones, and I will always be forever grateful.

At times, I know that their mom being gone was too heavy for kids their ages, but that is what goes through a mom's brain. Now, we call it "mom guilt," but at the time, I had no idea what it was or why I felt so torn. But the Herculean magnetic pull to be true to myself was what drew me to make choices in my life that would continue to keep me tethered to my true self—choices that would continue to shatter every possible limitation we impose on ourselves and allow society to impose on us. I feel that my choice was one that I needed and one that helped shape and weave the colorful fabric of my story and my family. My choice was one that forever ended the gender stereotype within my lineage, because guess what? It ended because I chose to go first, to do the scary, bold, audacious, and courageous thing: Live out the dream that had always been within my heart.

*woven*

# Chapter 15

# Lose Yourself to Find Yourself

SHERRI MARIE GAUDET

*Sherri Marie Gaudet*

Sherri Marie Gaudet is a 6x international best-selling author, founder of Mermaids and Mamas — a holistic skincare, clothing line, and women's empowerment community, host of the *Mermaids and Mamas* podcast, and mama to two amazing children. She believes you should always live in the moment because life is meant to be savored. Positive to a fault, she always finds a way to make things work, no matter the curve balls thrown her way. Sherri Marie always believed that nothing in the world was impossible, often doing her best work when the odds were stacked against her. Sherri Marie tried out many different career paths during her twenties before finally realizing that her talents were best spent helping others as an entrepreneur and business leader.

🌐 mermaidsandmamas.com

ⓕ mermaidsandmamas

📷 mermaidsandmamas

To my daughter's grandmother, Deb, who holds a special place in my heart for not only being the absolute best grandmother I could ask for but for also being such a special person in my life and teaching me so much, most especially, the value of love and hugs.

"Celebrate your strength. Bad chapters still create great stories. Wrong paths can always lead to the right places. Failed dreams can even make successful people. Sometimes it takes losing yourself to find yourself."

# Lose Yourself to Find Yourself

*She understands that the hardest times in life to go through were when you were transitioning from one version of yourself to another.*

–Sarah Addison Allen

*"Everything you experience in life is happening for you, not to you."* When I first heard this powerful statement in a personal development workshop a few years ago, I didn't fully grasp the power within this message. However, looking back at my life, it is one of the most profound statements anyone has ever shared with me.

Have you ever felt like your life was a never-ending series of WTFs? I know I have. There was a time where I even thought about getting it tattooed right across my forehead. I would wake up every morning and wonder, "Hmm . . . what is the universe going to dump on me today?" It seemed like there was always something *happening to me*. Looking back and reflecting on why things kept happening, the answer is so apparent and straightforward. I kept repeating the same mistakes over and over. I kept reliving the same patterns and cycles. I wasn't learning the lessons that I needed to learn or healing from past traumas and heartbreaks, so the universe kept sending me these curve balls until the lightbulb finally went off, and I had my aha moment. And even after I'd navigate every curve ball that came my way, I still didn't understand the underlying message that lay within each challenge. I would deal with the catastrophe of the moment and then continue along with the same life path, the same behavioral patterns. It wasn't until the universe finally had enough and tossed me a million curve balls all at once, instead of consecutively, that it hit me. *Bam!* I still resisted so hard. For months on end, I'd only deal with what I call the surface problems without ever examining the root cause.

I can't tell you how many tears were shed or miles were ran on the path to dry the tears. How many depressing days and sleepless nights I had. Or the countless family counseling sessions I've had alone, or with my daughter's father. I even wrote a ten-page letter to him before I finally realized it was me all along who needed to evolve, shift, and expand my perspective, my way of being. I have always been the positive one, the good friend who always saw the good in everything. However, I was also someone who was afraid to let anyone get too close to me. I wanted and needed to be loved; when I felt loved and secure, I was my best self. I had yet to discover how to give myself the same love and desire I craved from anyone else. However, I was so afraid of being hurt that I built substantial invisible walls that led to vicious repeat cycles in my life. My defense mechanisms were always engaged and ready to protect me, but instead of protecting me, they were hurting me. Even though I was still living life with my best qualities on the surface, subconsciously, my worst qualities continued to self-sabotage by never allowing anyone to get close to me. If they did, I would subconsciously push them away. I never even let my son get too close to me. We have what I like to refer to as more of a "friendship" than the typical mother–son bond. I operated this way for as long as I can remember until I had a "eureka" moment the size of a hurricane. This moment shifted everything for me, and I'll never be the same ever again, in the best way.

We all have life-altering moments that precede a significant life-changing, breakthrough moment. For me, this change came on a Tuesday morning when I called my daughter's grandmother, completely hysterical, and asked her, "But why? I'm trying so hard . . . I'm doing all the things I'm supposed to do . . . and I'm still failing." Her words were so warm and gentle; she didn't just tell me what I needed to do. Instead, she gently guided me to realize what I needed to do: I needed to deal with the root of all my troubles, which stemmed from having a very strained relationship with my mom my entire life.

I grew up having everything I could have ever hoped for or dreamed of having; I never had to go without. We were well taken care of and provided for. I'm very thankful for that, but I would have rather had more love and affection over materialistic things. Knowing me, you would think the opposite because I've always portrayed myself as being completely repulsed by affectionate behavior. In hindsight, I now realize that I always desired and longed for affection, but I built a façade to show that I was tough and didn't need any affection. Often, we keep our guard up; we harden our hearts and minds as a defense mechanism to protect ourselves from others and life. My doing so led to me always attracting the wrong types of men in my life, being taken advantage of at times in business, and ultimately raising my son entirely differently than I am now raising my daughter. My advice? Don't harden yourself, even when it hurts. Don't harden yourself, even when all logic dictates that you should. Permit yourself to feel, to hurt, and to heal. We can then learn to trust, let go, and let others become close with us. Those of us who portray that affection and love aren't our thing are often the ones who need it the most.

Change can be one of the scariest things you ever go through, especially when it comes to changing our behaviors and ways we live to "protect ourselves." However, if you aren't happy or keep reliving the same curve balls in life, you have to make life changes. You have to stop allowing yourself to be consumed by the fear of change. Stop allowing it to hold you back from doing things that could potentially change your life for the better. I have experienced many moments in my life where I feared change. I feared being a young mother who had no clue what she was doing. I feared being an entrepreneur. I feared buying a house all on my own. I then feared selling it and moving years later. I feared leaving a relationship in which I wasn't happy. Heck, for a long time, I feared allowing myself to fall genuinely in love with someone. When I reflect on my life thus far, while I made bold, courageous moves throughout, I did so with one foot rooted deep in fear while the other continued to move forward with resistance.

A few months ago, my daughter's grandmother, who holds such a special place in my heart, sat me down and told me that I was an amazing mom and an incredible person who had so much love to give, but that I, too, needed to be loved and shown affection. She said that the universe sends us exactly what we need and what we are ready for at the exact time we need it and are prepared to have it in our life. That life always works out, sometimes even better than you can imagine it will. She told me that I needed to send out to the universe what I wanted and, even more importantly, be open and prepared to receive exactly what I asked from the universe when it responds. She didn't know when or how it would happen, but she was sure someone would come into my life and show me the love and affection I always wanted, as long as I allowed it to happen. She was 100 percent right, and that is why my results this time, though it's still newer, are turning out to be everything I always dreamed of having.

When my daughter's grandmother was teaching me about love and being open to finding it, I don't think she was referring to her son. Perhaps she was, without telling me, because she wanted me to figure that part out on my own. When we first started having our heart-to-heart conversations, and I started learning how to be open to love and affection, her son wasn't the first person to cross my mind. Even though we share our daughter, who we both love unconditionally, we were both just focused on being incredible co-parents. Neither one of us looked at the other as our "ideal match," and perhaps that is why neither of us were successful in our previous relationships. The one thing we always shared was that "love and affection weren't our things," but deep down, it was what we both craved and needed. As my daughter's grandmother taught me more about love and relationships, I started mentally making a list of the qualities I wanted in a man, and I slowly started realizing that the universe was screaming at me to open my eyes. The answer was right in front of me. I realized that when I described my ideal guy, I kept describing my daughter's father.

It wasn't a eureka moment where I then picked up the phone

*woven*

and said, "OMG! We are imperfectly perfect for each other." It was something that I realized gradually, and in doing so, I also realized I was open to it. I didn't force it, and I didn't exactly have a plan. Instead, I let life happen with an open mind and an open heart. I allowed things to naturally flow without overthinking them and, most importantly, without pushing them away and building a wall. And no, we didn't live *happily ever after* . . . we live with beautiful imperfections that are perfect to us both. Our days aren't flawless or perfect. I have no idea if, in the long term, we will become a family again or whether our time together is just another chapter of lessons from the universe. However, what I do know is that by doing things differently this time around, my results are different. My experience is that much more powerful and unique. I feel like a different woman—a woman able to hold it all: the grief, sadness, joy, love, comfort, hurt, anger, uncertainty, and desire. I'm allowing life to flow naturally without any resistance. And flow state has been my favorite state. It feels like coming home to myself and relaxing in the comfort of my power, of my worth, of my own self-love and acknowledging that my desires matter. I matter. And I am worthy of giving myself love and affection while allowing myself to receive that from those around me as well.

One of the greatest things my daughter's grandmother taught me was the importance of a simple hug. Something so simple can be so powerful and important and totally change how you experience the rest of your day. Now, if I'm being completely honest, I was as awkward as they come with hugs. I didn't know how to give or receive them without them feeling forced and just plain awkward. Yet, they always did feel amazing to receive, and deep down, I craved them. Like anything else in life, what you give is what you receive. So naturally, when I stopped sending signals to the universe that I hated something and instead let it know that I was open to new things, hugs, too, became less awkward and, dare I say, natural.

The past year has been life changing. In fact, when I reflect on my life, I am so proud of the woman I have been, the woman I had to become, and the woman I am becoming so that I can change the way my daughter and I experience life moving forward. Life always works out. Remember this truth when you feel like you're in a hard place or feel like you are being challenged the most. Believe in where you are headed. See the bigger picture of what lies ahead of you instead of what you're leaving behind. You may look at your current situation right now and feel desperate, defeated, and lost. That's not permanent, though. Tell yourself these words: **Whatever it is, it will pass. And you don't have to do it on your own.** Take a course, hire a coach, learn how to self-coach, go to a workshop, read an insane number of books. Work on your mindset every day because whether you believe you can or can't, you are 100 percent right. Shifting how we look at things takes time and practice. There is a lesson in every situation. The more challenging something is, the more growth we will experience. Growth isn't supposed to be easy. It is supposed to stretch you to a new level. It's supposed to feel like rebirth, because it is. Change never happens inside your comfort zone.

Every page of our life holds something new, exciting, intriguing, adventurous, enlightening, and emotional. Don't ever get stuck on a page; turn the page, see what is next, and you may be surprised. Remember, this is your story. The ups and downs, they are yours; embrace them. Be proud of how you've handled challenging times. The silent battles you fought, the moments you had to humble yourself, wipe your tears and pat yourself on the back. Celebrate your strength. Bad chapters still create great stories. Wrong paths can always lead to the right places. Failed dreams can even make successful people. Sometimes it takes losing yourself to find yourself.

# Chapter 16

# Tales of Dragons, Success, and Motherhood

EMILY EDWARDS

*Emily Edwards*

Emily Edwards, RN, BScN, is a multi-passionate person on a mission to change the culture of care. By trade she is a nurse, but her dynamic and eclectic career path, motherhood, and random interests have pushed her to help others in the ways the traditional health care system has missed their needs. Dismantling the systems that never served the people drives *everything* she does.

Emily grew up in a small Ontario city where the exposure to diversity was minimal. As a parent now raising three Black children with her spouse, she has placed antiracism work as a priority in her life.

She is the visionary behind The Good Birth Co., an online space that provides full-spectrum pregnancy, birth, and postpartum support. She left the grind of shiftwork and the nine-to-five nurse life to help people create the birth experience they want or process the one they didn't. By placing her personal core values of radical empathy, barrier elimination, and storytelling at the heart of her work, she has intentionally cultivated a community that is moving the mission forward with her.

When Emily isn't asking big questions or coaching others to do the same, she is likely listening to a playlist full of old school and early 2000's hip-hop. She's obsessed with dog training and can discuss dog breeds for hours. Additionally, she is navigating how to live with complex chronic health diagnoses and chronic pain that lead to frustration and fatigue.

🌐 thegoodbirthco.com

📷 @thegoodbirthco


For three very important people and groups: myself, the people I've hurt, and the people who showed up. For Emily: You did it. You are a published author. I am infinitely proud of you. For the friendships I've lost: I am sorry I didn't take better care of us. I'm deeply sorry I lost you along the way. And for those of you who showed up, this chapter is for you. For us.

"*Here's the thing*. The princess stories and realities of our mothers didn't leave room for the most important truth. No one spoke up and shared their true fear for new parents."

# Tales of Dragons, Success, and Motherhood

*I write for those women who do not speak, for those who do not have a voice because they were so terrified, because we are taught to respect fear more than ourselves. We've been taught that silence would save us, but it won't.*

–Audre Lorde

This is where the story begins. With me sitting on top of the world. I was in love and flying to follow my life's passion. *I was spending the next six weeks catching babies in a busy labor and delivery ward in the capital city of Tanzania.*

In the spring of 2011, I sat on a flight destined for the continent of Africa. My striped notebook sat open on my lap, and I remember thinking, *This will make the perfect start of a book one day . . .*

This moment, obviously, was the starting point of success.

I was adventurous.

I was clever.

I was driven.

I was full of ambition and promise.

I was what *Girl Power* dreams were made of.

And then I became pregnant.

That was when the world traded my ambition for resilience.

And it was my birth experience that killed my dreams of success and left me feeling like a failure.

So, this is where the story really begins:

There is a dragon inside of me now where ambition and drive and purpose live. A dragon seething, smoldering for escape. You see, I was lured into the cage too; the promise of goodness and success were irresistible. *I was a good girl.*

But I chased the promise into the snare society had laid long ago and waited for me.

I know your longing and the relentless desire to be seen for your entire self. The you who exists now. Not the one they expected to meet when you grew into an adult. The one who is too real for this world.

I see your bravery, and I know how you earned it. Woven are

our stories; we have entirely different lives, but I see the crimson thread holding you together. It's a warning and a welcome, all at once. *I am here,* it shouts to me. I can see it frayed at one end. I see the twisted tail on the other, gently spun between your thumb and forefinger. Around and around and around. Comfort.

I have one of those threads too. It holds me together: the shattered pieces, the rage, and the dragon searching for escape.

The world threatens you with attacks because it has no other answers once you give up carrying its narrative. Your character. Your body. Your integrity. Your intelligence. Your capabilities. It feels as if you are open to all attacks. You chose this. Motherhood. You got trapped in the snare. This was your choice.

You see, the darkness that sits where ambition and drive and purpose live has a yearning of its own. It seeks only one thing: justice.

None of it disappeared. All the things that the world assumed would lead to my inevitable success still exist in me, albeit a little bit differently.

I am a secret keeper. And I always have been. I am the place people feel safe sharing their deepest, darkest feelings. My grandmother was a secret keeper too. But it wasn't until feeling the emptiness of a traumatic birth and eventually discovering the vocabulary to address it that I could name my own darkness.

As a keeper of secrets, I know there is beauty in the depths of our soul. In the shadows and recesses where our stories get buried.

While much of our stories intersect, bumping off each other throughout our lives, nothing ties my heart to yours more than knowing you share the darkness too. You have felt the sting of loneliness that accompanies entering motherhood and facing the scary things you have kept buried.

The effort I will go to avoid failure is where most of my darkness lurks. I believed avoiding failure as a new parent was accomplishing an intervention-free home birth; my first birth experience was the opposite. I failed out of the gates.

I had visualized my birth ideal over and over in my mind. I was ready for a beautiful home birth, surrounded by my closest supports. Success matters in any arena when you *live for it*. My birth experience would be a success. And there was no Plan B.

It ended up anything but intervention-free. I experienced what is known as *the cascade of interventions* that lead to a cesarean birth. And I was left broken by the loss of control.

Certainly, if an intervention-free birth was the stuff birth success stories were made of, I wasn't going to make the cut. The kind yet condescending words I received as condolences after my oldest was born replicated the other well-meaning people in my life up until this point in my pregnancy.

The look they gave me was all the same. *Oh, what a smart girl. It's too bad. You really did try; it was a bit too ambitious, that's all.*

I was a good girl. I followed the rules. I effortlessly met expectations. I thrived on positive feedback. It came plentifully; I was labeled as an exceptional child in elementary school, and I sailed through my high school years on a fast track for *success*. I never knew what I wanted to be when I grew up. But I knew I wanted to be *successful*. The world around me reinforced this concept. I even have the prom '08 award to prove it. *Most Likely to Succeed.*

I laugh at the irony . . . *What did success look like at seventeen years old?*

Success felt like perfection. It tasted like victory. It was being exceptional.

I was sold on the dream: the education, the career, the house, the husband, the kids. The Dream.

It was always someone else's construct of success. It was meeting external criteria to appear *successful*. It was the avoidance of feeling shame, guilt, and embarrassment. It wasn't focused on meeting my own needs and feeling fulfilled.

I was fortunate that my gifted abilities in reading and comprehension and interpersonal skills made meeting expectations easy. But what happens when you have abilities like that? It is easy to avoid failure. It wasn't that I feared failure, it was that I didn't know how to fail. I had no coping skills to maneuver through the feelings that accompanied failing. I sobbed after failing my first driving test.

The part I forgot to mention was avoiding writing the first test to even *begin the driving process* for almost a year. I knew learning the skills to drive a car would be difficult for me. It wasn't as simple as *reading and memorizing it*. I avoided the possibility of failing. And I failed anyway.

My version of success always included *the kids*. My end goal was always to have kids of my own. Actually, my biggest fear was waiting until after chasing my wild dreams and being unable to conceive or carry children of my own. I also didn't imagine myself being an older parent.

I also carried a false sense of ability when it came to parenting. I was a popular nanny and took on challenging assignments. I was a stellar nanny. I believed those skills would transfer over easily into my own parenthood journey. But I was a piece of a system that supported those families to thrive. I missed the strategy that contributed to their *success*. They have built in support where the world is failing us.

I learned quickly that in a world that championed the construct of family . . . it fails mothers.

But no one mentioned this fact to me. Ever. I was raised on Disney princesses and by women who *worked*. I was going to have it all, and they wanted that for me too. *All* included the career, the spouse, the kids . . . *remember?*

Here's the thing: The princess stories and realities of our mothers didn't leave room for the *most important truth*. No one spoke up and shared their true fear for new parents. No one ever spoke the biggest secret in motherhood (except for hemorrhoids, that is) out loud.

Society would fail me, and I would struggle to keep up . . .

At no fault of my own or due to a deficit tied directly to *being a mother*. I beat myself up for obtaining the dream out of order. My family began in 2011 when I got pregnant with my oldest. My now-husband and I hadn't been dating very long, and to say it was a shock to everyone I knew is an understatement.

"The baby before marriage must be the reason it's so hard," I would tell myself. But the fact was, it was being pregnant at all that made it harder. The systems I existed within did not want to see a pregnant person achieve their goals.

We never learned about the day-to-day reality of the motherhood tax and the unrecognized double-shift our mothers endured. *Ambition* usually died a tragic death somewhere within the massive gap where their career once was. Even those of us who had mothers setting badass examples in so many ways—they did a remarkable job making it look easy.

The fact was that I was becoming a mother before my career began. I didn't know about the motherhood tax. I thought the playing field was reasonably level. And no one had the heart to tell it to me straight.

Our society is hyper-focused on the proliferation of the hetero-normative, traditional family. While this definition is broadening, it is still assumed that you're in a relationship with someone of the opposite sex and of the same race. And you are in a monogamous relationship . . . preferably married. Outside of this experience, pregnancy is not celebrated in the same ways. There is something taboo about pregnancy, even in today's world.

The fact was I was a third-year university student working toward my nursing degree. Only a few months before learning I was pregnant, I had won a scholarship for excellence in academic and clinical performance. I carried an over 90 percent grade average in a rigorous program. *I already proved to everyone that I was capable. They cheered me on pursuing my wildest dreams. But . . . why were they so worried about me becoming a mother? Wasn't that part of the plan?*

I understand now it wasn't *me* they didn't believe in. They just knew the harsh reality. Motherhood makes it harder. I would be forced to be able to withstand or recover quickly from difficult conditions. I would become *resilient.* The pursuit of success would fall to the wayside; there would be no more time to overestimate your abilities. Resilience is about survival, not pursuing self-development and excellence.

The world around me didn't believe in me. Suddenly I no longer was the clever, ambitious, young woman destined for big things. I was the resilient pregnant girl, fighting her way to graduate.

I was not used to my ability being questioned. The gossip and questioning came from people I anticipated unwavering support from. These were the adults who had known me my entire life, who had helped raise me and guide me and believed in me the most.

It disappeared the instant they heard I was pregnant. The gossip and the questions my own parents were berated with: *Emily? Are you sure? What is she going to do? But she worked so hard. What about her education? What is she going to do?*

My mom joked with me and said, "If you hear through the grapevine that you've dropped out of school, it started with me. It feels like that's what everyone is anticipating hearing."

*Funny, I expected support.*

How wrong I was. I suppose the reality of a fierce person becoming a mother is that we become even more ferocious. Aside from small town gossip, I learned firsthand the efforts the world goes to in order to make life difficult for parents while I battled for accommodation throughout my entire pregnancy. The nursing department refused to support me in pursuing completing full-time studies while pregnant. It fell on my shoulders to advocate for myself.

My entire pregnancy I was met with the belief that I had made the wrong choice in becoming a parent. *Silly little girl* was the feeling I got from most of the world around me. However, at the end of that very long ten months, I looked into the face of a physician who solidified the vibe I had been feeling my entire pregnancy. "You tried," she said to me as she patted my foot, "but this baby just doesn't want to come."

I was already in shock. My body and mind had withstood an immense amount of stress my entire pregnancy. I felt the impact and reality of being pregnant in a world that is set up for a very narrow version of the family. Here I was, becoming a parent and being told how my child would be born. Out of my control. Silly little girl, your dreams were too big. My goals for birth were even too ambitious. *I can't be both*. I was defeated.

I never want to be resilient again. I want to be passionate, capable, and driven. I want the world to believe in me the way it did before I became pregnant.

People called me resilient. Even more so after that point. They stopped calling me ambitious and bright altogether then.

I decided to redefine that story.

What processing my birth experience taught me was that I was capable of facing my biggest fears. I was capable of experiencing the loss of control that terrified me, to withstand the unfair treatment because I did not fit the mold, to own where I did not show up perfectly, but to also acknowledge where I showed up in the best way I could. Moving through the guilt, resentment, and feelings

*woven*

of failure that clouded the memories of my birth story allowed me to celebrate my truly triumphant entry into parenthood.

It did not fit the narrow version of success I had allowed myself to envision; it was bigger than that. It was a major life transition that deserved respect, honor, and true recognition.

I never wanted to be celebrated as resilient. I wanted to be ambitious and a mother.

It has taken me my entire parenting journey to say that (well, type that) out loud. **I want to be both.** I deserve to pursue and achieve the success my wildest dreams are made of, except now I am the one who defines them. It is no longer an ambiguous end destination or "ever present state of mind." I have the right to define my own success and pursue it while existing as a parent and raising my children with help from the world around me.

My birth experience taught me that there is space for both. Grief and joy. Pain and pleasure. Fear and hope. Tenacity and gentleness. Capability and support. It taught me that my intuition and patience are powerful but I need to protect them.

I now know the biggest secret. The world is terrified of the mother. The human woven together into the flesh of humanity. Crimson is the thread that ties the pieces of power and pain and fear and triumph together. Frayed and tired at one end. Smooth, familiar, comfortable at the other as it rolls between thumb and forefinger. And a *supported* mother is unstoppable. No wonder it is impossibly hard to *do it all*. The world is afraid of us and makes it hard to own our needs.

It isn't the way we bear children that births solidarity among us, it's the triumph of survival, of knowing we are still here despite the journey taken thus far. And owning what happens next.

I reject society getting to label us passionate, fire-filled humans as merely strong despite the challenges we've overcome instead of who we have always been. Yes. I am a mother. But I was so much more than that long before that became a part of me.

I want to be brave because of my adventures in Tanzania.

I want to be ferocious because of my advocacy for others.

I want to be bright because I solve problems others cannot.

I don't want to be resilient anymore. I am ready to be who I have always been. The dragon can stay, though.

And together, woven with the vestiges of all my experiences, the dragon and I set out to slay more demons every day—expectations, perfection, the façades we are expected to cloak ourselves in *for their comfort*. No more. No more. No more. I am a dragoness, and within me lies a burning passion that will not be quelled. A *me* that continues to burn bright and hold this torch for my fellow dragonesses to see so they, too, no longer quell their passion and fire at the sacrificial altar of a world that continues to exalt and dethrone the very women who continue to birth multiple worlds within them and of them.

*woven*

The dragon can stay, for she is needed. She is within every one of us who've bound ourselves to this call with the crimson thread of womanhood and motherhood that binds us together.

# *Chapter 17*

# An Invocation, Imramma, and Imara

TANIA JANE MORAES-VAZ

*Tania Jane Moraes-Vaz*

Tania Jane Maraes-Vaz is a woman of many capes — wife, mom, mentor, and friend. She is a self-expression expert, multi-best-selling author, creative maven and content creator, and podcast host who helps women uncover and express their unique stories in a way that is compelling and authentic to them. After losing her way for a brief three years post-grad while working in corporate hedge funds, fintech, and marketing, she can finally say, "Look, Ma, I'm actually using my English degree." Like Alice ventured down the rabbit hole, Tania found her way back to her soul-calling of storytelling and self-expression through a series of "yes" ventures in the world of writing and publishing. These "yes" ventures led Tania to fuse her passion for creativity, holistic healing, photography, and writing, and she birthed Warrior Life Creative Co — a holistic, full-scale creative agency specializing in energy marketing using mentorship, energetic healing, strategy, and white-glove service — creating an ALL-IN-ONE for heart-inspired entrepreneurs and brands. She is also a creative partner and developmental editor at YGTMedia Co. and co-founder of *Mama Brain Magazine* with her biz bestie, Sabrina Greer. When Tania isn't busy putting out fires or igniting you into wildfire self-expression, she is building Lego with her family, cozying up with a cuppa and some good books, or envisioning world domination where every creative is fully self-expressed. Her goal: No creative left behind. No voice left unexpressed.

🌐 **warriorlifecreativeco.com**

📷 **@warriorlifecreative**

To you, dear reader. May you never stop shining your light. May you never stop being YOU.

"I am woman. I am a warrioress. I am a creatrix. I birth life and I nurture it. Within me lies the power to destroy anything that threatens the very existence of this delicate balance—this fiery tango of divine masculine and feminine."

# An Invocation, Imramma, and Imara

Throughout this book, there have been themes of homecoming, finding oneself amid the chaos, learning to advocate for one's own needs. Themes of disruption, oppression, and a renewed sense of fight to be seen, to be heard, to listen to our intuition.

Though the world around us is evolving rapidly, and there are so many unknowns that we are surrounded with in each moment, may you always come back to your center, to the calm that lies within you, to the fire that burns bright within you.

Allow yourself to embark on a journey of a lifetime. Allow yourself to grow over a lifetime, to love over a lifetime, to become exactly who you are meant to be, over a lifetime.

There is no race to be won, just your own.

There are no timelines that matter, just the one you choose for yourself.

There are glimpses of your Muse that you'll receive ever so often; allow her into your life. She is you. My muse, Imara, visits me often: in my dreams, while I'm simply being, or other times while I'm in my chaos of life, wifehood, motherhood, and being a businesswoman. She wears many different capes, many different kaftans, and she has a sultry, fiery presence. Other times she feels like a mother's hug on a lonely, heavy day, or a lover's caress on a day where desires are abundant and require attention. And sometimes, she's very much a playful child who beckons me to come out and play, get silly with my son, roll around in the grass, and just smell the magic around me.

## Imara's Invocation

Your love

Your loss.

Your pride.

Your fall.

Your tears, your laughter. And the mirth hidden in every faint smile.

*woven*

Take me with you

On your stairway to success.

Your climb up your mountains.

The scrapes and tumbles.

The hurdles and omens.


Take me with you

Through your inner musings

The desires and longings

Just one more time.


Take me with you

Here I belong.

Here I hear my calling.

Here I find myself free falling.

Into love.

Obsession.

Trust.

Expansion.

Here I find, ME.


Never let me go.

Not now.

Not ever.

You and me, we're one and the same.

Bound together. Bound forever.

In our pain and healing.

Our cup of intoxicating pleasure and possibility.

You and me, forever. Never without. Never again.

We find our way back to each other,

Through the grief, the pain, the illusions, the lies, and more.

Never let me go.


Take me with you.

Into your flow.

Into your free falling.

Into your soul expansion.

For you are me, and I am you.

Here I am, ready for more—adventure, calling, culling,

evolving, rising, mother, crone, goddess, Me, You. Us.

✶✶✶

Collectively, as women, as humans, we are one—our blood bleeds the same, our tears carry the same saltiness, our heart stirs with nuanced emotion that we can all identify with, no matter where we come from, what our socioeconomic or cultural background may be.

It is my sincere hope that within each of these stories, within each of these women in this book, you find a facet of yourself that is now heard and seen.

That no matter the obstacles you face, no matter the paths you choose to venture on, you always choose yourself. Choose your dreams. Choose your vision. And align with it. When you build a life based on the vision that is true to you in every way, everything around you aligns accordingly.

## An Immram

Immram: An immram is a class of Old Irish tales concerning a hero's sea journey to the Otherworld. Written in the Christian era and essentially Christian in aspect, they preserve elements of Irish mythology.

There once was a girl, Imara.
Heart full of dreams
Head full of screams.
Theirs, hers.
Hush . . . for a moment, all is still.

As she grew older,
Heart full of love
Head full of armor.

Theirs, hers.

Lay it down—that guarded veil, that heavy, ironclad armor.

No, I can't. Even today, I can't seem to do that.


Heart full of desire, passion, lust even.

Head full of insults.

Body full of battle scars

Seen and unseen.


As she transitioned from maiden to mother,

Who will make love to you?

You're fat.

You're ugly.

You're scarred.

You're marked.

You're tainted.

Assaulted.

Beaten.

Black. Blue, and every hue.

Marks that fade, but you can feel it.

The debris of energy. The turmoil. The constant battle.

To be enough.

To be worthy.

To be me.

*woven*

Until one day, she couldn't take it anymore.

Blade in one hand, good-bye letters all written.

Signed and sealed.

She heard cry that shook her out of her silent reverie.

They'll probably be happy that I'm gone.

The cry continued, louder. Mama, are you sad? Mama,
where are you?

Clang! Blade dropping to the ground, her cheeks wet with
tears and grief, she felt her Creator pull her out of this
trance.

Her angels and Muse, she could feel them.

Imara, your Heart is full of big, bold, fiery visions.

Even if your Head is full of endless questions.

Hush . . . for a moment, heart and head are one.

Pause. Look how far you've come.

Look how much you've evolved.

Look at the foundation that your life has been built on.

Look at the crown of thorns that you wear,

Gracefully.

Divine light shining through you.

For you, my dear, were destined for greatness.

And these were the cups you were chosen to drink from.

Cups that were overflowing with experiences only you could
teach from.

And she rose. And so it is. She continues, to this day, to rise. To sit with the battle between Heart and Head, and guess what wins out every time? What has never led her astray? Heart. And guess what has helped her foresee, envision, and bring it to fruition? Head. Together, the three of them make a sultry tango that mesmerizes everyone who cannot help but watch.

She is me. She is you. She is us.
You are Museworthy. You are Worthy. You are created from Divine stardust, intention, and love. Do you still think your experiences have no meaning, no purpose? Do you still think you have no purpose? Shine on.

### Lines in the Sand

And just when you think
You almost lost it all,
Your identity, your strength, your soul
Your all,
Your Self.
You found Her.

You found Her standing there,

Gazing at you, lovingly asking you,

"What took you so long? I've been watching you . . . rise and fall. Sabotage. Over and over.

I've been waiting for you. Waiting for you to get out of your own way. For you to finally start believing in me: your Self. I've got your back. Do you have your back?"


You realized in that moment, you were standing at a precipice. Swaying. Teetering on the brink of expansion. A defining moment.

A fine line in the sand.

They say you can either draw this line or people will draw it for you.

And the thing with allowing anyone else to draw that line for you is this: You are powerless, forever at their mercy.

What a powerless state of being!

Why choose that when you have the power to be/do/have anything you desire?

Why give away your power and your soul when you can harness it to create sheer magic in your life? When you can light the way, forge the path, and heal with your medicine? When you have been destined to go first?

So, wild one, lean in.

To yourself.

Lean into your fire, your sparks, your moments where you feel fierce, magnetic, and unapologetic.

The moments where you feel beautiful, even through the mess of it all.

Xoxo,
Tania Jane

*woven*

# Shadows

Owning your shadows will set you free.

It will be your source of power and strength.


I used to feel so ashamed.

I used to feel so broken.

I used to feel so freaking afraid.

Of always being the one who talks a lot.

Of always being the one who is positive and chooses to see things in an optimistic light.

Of always being trusting and open, even after going through many betrayals in various forms.

Of procrastinating because my best ideas often come under pressure (healthy pressure I must add).

I was ashamed and embarrassed of
My health condition and the challenges that came with it.
Of my downward spirals.
Of my anxious and depressed episodes that lasted days, sometimes weeks.
Of wanting to be seen, to be heard and understood.
Of feeling afraid of myself, my thoughts, who I am as a person.
Where I've been, what I've done, what I've been through.
Of being equally culpable of my own undoing in many different situations.
Of giving away my power, my trust.
Of drowning out my voice.
Of resisting my need to rest or take it slow some days.
Of listening to those chills in my bones.
Of tuning into that voice within me.
Of mothering that child within me.
Of honoring that wise woman within me.

Until one day, where I could no longer be ashamed, no longer be afraid.

*woven*

Until I could no longer hide behind my shield of being "broken."

Instead, I chose to make it my cape. I chose to own it.

To wear it loud and proud. To feel into it and find strength and grace in all the fractures, all the crevices, all jarring dualities of myself.

And so it was. And so it is.

Owning your light and your dark is your unique blueprint.

It will help you be fearless despite your fear and help you evolve faster than you ever thought possible.

Face your darkest truths. Own your power.

Turn your fears into your source of strength and light.

The best part about owning your truth, your shadow, your darkness. It no longer holds power over you.

That voice in your head cannot win anymore, for you have confronted your darkest fears, faced your feelings instead of numbing away and hiding away.


You look them in the eye every day, heck every minute, if that's what it takes.

You befriend them, you embrace those demons and acknowledge they are there to teach you something.

You become more self-aware and gain an awareness of those around you.

You teach yourself how to embrace both the light and dark that exists within you and choose to transmute it into pure radiant, bright strength.

You are a warrior who continues your fight for life fiercely and unwaveringly.

*woven*

# Works Cited

## Chapter 1 by Chiara Fritzler

Kierkegaard, Soren. *Either/Or: A Fragment of Life*. Penguin revised ed., 1992.

## Chapter 5 by Sara Costa

Chanel, Coco. *The Gospel According to Coco Chanel: Life Lessons from the World's Most Elegant Woman*. skirt!, 2009.

## Chapter 9 by Leanne Ford

1. Postpartum Support International - PSI. (2021, April 26). https://www.postpartum.net/

2. 20123 Postpartum Depression. CAMH. (n.d.). https://www.camh.ca/en/health-info/mental-illness-and-addiction-index/postpartum-depression.

## Chapter 13 by Jennifer De Rossi

1. J.P. Pierce et al., "Greater Survival After Breast Cancer in Physically Active Women with High Vegetable-Fruit Intake Regardless of Obesity," Journal of Clinical Oncology 25, no. 17 (June 2007): 2345-51

YGTMedia Co. is a blended boutique publishing house for mission-driven humans. We help seasoned and emerging authors "birth their brain babies" through a supportive and collaborative approach. Specializing in narrative nonfiction and adult and children's empowerment books, we believe that words can change the world, and we intend to do so one book at a time.

ygtmedia.co/publishing
@ygtmedia.co
@ygtmedia.co